WHAT YOUR COLLEAGUES ARE SAYING . . .

"This book is a game changer. This step-by-step manual for establishing collective efficacy that fosters student learning is absolutely necessary in education—not just in this current environment, but always. There's something for everyone in this book. It's relevant for district leaders—even school boards, principals, coaches, and classroom teachers. The actionable steps in this book are not grade-level specific. They work for all grade levels, all content areas, all schools everywhere. It contains opportunities in every chapter to respond, reflect, collaborate, and set goals that will make schools better. Everyone wins when the steps outlined throughout this book are taken—administrators, teachers, students—everyone wins. This is more than a feel-good book, more than a book full of lessons—it's a resource that makes collective efficacy attainable. *Collaborating Through Collective Efficacy Cycles* could just prompt an educator's revival."

—**Elaine Shobert,** Literacy Coach and Lead Teacher
Rock Rest Elementary School, Monroe, NC

"This text really advocates for authentic, meaningful professional learning experiences in-house that honor the teacher. *Collaborating Through Collective Efficacy Cycles* will resonate with and meet the needs of many educators. The clear process shared is powerful because it can be used across grade levels. It really works for *all* teams. Our teachers are our greatest source of professional development and giving them this roadmap to improve practice is essential."

—**Katie McGrath,** Instructional Facilitator
Loudoun County Public Schools, Aldie, VA

"For those of us working on high-quality instruction and developing teacher capacity, this text presents the PLC process as a well-framed, well-explained, and well-attained growth cycle for our teachers. *Collaborating Through Collective Efficacy Cycles* takes on a topic that many schools have had mixed results with. This playbook essentially guides educators with action steps. Many readers have had some experience with a version of a PLC in their district, but it is safe to say that this provides a more systematic approach in tapping into teacher leadership."

—**Michael Rafferty,** Director of Teaching and Learning
Derby Public Schools, Derby, CT

COLLABORATING THROUGH COLLECTIVE EFFICACY CYCLES

COLLABORATING THROUGH COLLECTIVE EFFICACY CYCLES

ENSURING ALL STUDENTS AND TEACHERS SUCCEED

A PLAYBOOK

INCLUDES
35+
VIDEOS

TONI FADDIS
DOUGLAS FISHER
NANCY FREY

CORWIN
Fisher & Frey

FOR INFORMATION:

Corwin

A SAGE Company

2455 Teller Road

Thousand Oaks, California 91320

(800) 233-9936

www.corwin.com

SAGE Publications Ltd.

1 Oliver's Yard

55 City Road

London EC1Y 1SP

United Kingdom

SAGE Publications India Pvt. Ltd.

B 1/I 1 Mohan Cooperative Industrial Area

Mathura Road, New Delhi 110 044

India

SAGE Publications Asia-Pacific Pte. Ltd.

18 Cross Street #10-10/11/12

China Square Central

Singapore 048423

President: Mike Soules

Vice President and
  Editorial Director: Monica Eckman

Director and Publisher,
  Corwin Classroom: Lisa Luedeke

Senior Content Development
  Manager: Julie Nemer

Associate Content
  Development Editor: Sarah Ross

Editorial Assistant: Nancy Chung

Production Editor: Melanie Birdsall

Typesetter: C&M Digitals (P) Ltd.

Proofreader: Lawrence W. Baker

Cover Designer: Gail Buschman

Marketing Manager: Deena Meyer

Printed in Canada

ISBN 978-1-0718-8862-9

This book is printed on acid-free paper.

22 23 24 25 26 10 9 8 7 6 5 4 3 2 1

CONTENTS

MODULE 4: COLLABORATIVE PLANNING AND SAFE PRACTICE

MODULE 5: COLLABORATIVE PLANNING AND OPENING UP PRACTICE

Visit the companion website at
resources.corwin.com/collectiveefficacy
for videos and downloadable resources.

LIST OF VIDEOS

Note From the Publisher: The authors have provided video and web content throughout the book that is available to you through QR (quick response) codes. To read a QR code, you must have a smartphone or tablet with a camera. We recommend that you download a QR code reader app that is made specifically for your phone or tablet brand.

Videos may also be accessed at **resources.corwin.com/collectiveefficacy**

ACKNOWLEDGMENTS

Corwin gratefully acknowledges the contributions of the following reviewers and educators:

Denise Finney
Educator
Chula Vista Elementary School District
Chula Vista, CA

Krista Geffre
Graduate Instructor
The Innovative Northwest Teacher
Hillsboro, OR

Giulia Longo
Educator
Chula Vista Elementary School District
Chula Vista, CA

Beverly Prange
Principal
Chula Vista Elementary School District
Chula Vista, CA

Michael Rafferty
Director of Teaching and Learning
Derby Public Schools
Derby, CT

Elaine Shobert
Literacy Coach and Lead Teacher
Rock Rest Elementary School
Monroe, NC

Christopher Turner
Educator
Chula Vista Elementary School District
Chula Vista, CA

INTRODUCTION

Have you heard of *collective teacher efficacy?* This term is widely used in educational circles, but you may be wondering, "What does efficacy really mean? It sounds good, but how does it happen?" Others may be concerned that it's yet another thing on an already full plate. Collective teacher efficacy is the "perception of teachers in a school that the efforts of the faculty as a whole will have a positive effect on students" (Goddard et al., 2000, p. 480). This playbook demystifies the concept of collective teacher efficacy and offers a defined pathway toward educators' personal and professional fulfillment, while simultaneously elevating student achievement and well-being.

Let's break this concept apart. From Bandura's (1977) early work on social cognitive theory, we understand that people want to have some level of control over their lives. When an individual experiences this sense of control, they feel a sense of *self-efficacy.* Self-efficacy is the "belief in one's capabilities to organize and execute a course of action" (Bandura, 1997, p. 3) that leads to a desired result. Since people interact with others through a network of relationships, we understand that *collective efficacy* is a group's shared belief that by working together they have the capacity to successfully organize and execute a course of action. In schools, *collective teacher efficacy* is the belief that efforts of teachers working together—as a collective, rather than as individuals—are capable of positively impacting student learning and motivation.

> **Self-efficacy is the "belief in one's capabilities to organize and execute a course of action."**

A RUNNER'S HIGH

If you've ever completed a long run and felt like you could keep going a few more miles, you may have experienced a runner's high. It's a feeling of bliss and excitement that occurs when a runner hits a certain stride. People who play other sports or exercise with intensity may also feel a runner's high when they get into a rhythm or groove. In this case, the euphoric feeling occurs after intense exercise, but others experience a similar sensation when they're on a winning team or playing music in perfect rhythm with a band or orchestra. There is newfound energy, a second wind. If you've felt this sensation before, you know that your head feels clear and your entire being seems lighter. You're in a groove, a zone, or state of flow (e.g., Csikszentmihalyi, 1990).

◄ OVERVIEW OF THE
COLLECTIVE EFFICACY CYCLE
resources.corwin.com/collectiveefficacy

To read a QR code, you must have a smartphone or tablet with a camera. We recommend that you download a QR code reader app that is made specifically for your phone or tablet brand.

This mental state, a state of flow and inner harmony, can be cultivated by teachers who work collaboratively toward a shared goal and attain it.

There are mental benefits that stem from collective teacher efficacy. These benefits don't just happen by chance, though, just as the mere act of running doesn't promise a runner's high. We may run several miles each day but still feel awkward and out of breath at the end of each run. Instead, the right conditions must be present to feel the sensation. We must train in specific ways to create the best conditions for the runner's high to manifest.

◄ NANCY SHARES ABOUT
COLLECTIVE FLOW
resources.corwin.com/collectiveefficacy

The same holds true for teaching, although teachers may not be aware that feeling this sensation is possible for people who work in schools. This could be because, like recreational runners, teachers may not train in optimal ways. What might happen if we trained with more intention by systematically designing collaborative professional learning experiences? The answer is we could increase the likelihood for the runner's high to appear for each member of the collaborative group. Essentially, we could create collective flow, or co-flow. Collective flow is a "state that occurs when a group is performing at the peak of its abilities" (Sawyer, 2003, p. 167). There is empirical evidence that collective flow occurs from the combination of high challenges and high skills (Salanova et al., 2014).

> High skills × high challenge + success = collective teacher efficacy

Teaching has long been viewed as an individual activity. In this playbook, we contend that teaching *and learning* can be more effective when teachers work together. While individuals can develop a degree of confidence and self-efficacy working alone, greater confidence, self-efficacy, and collective efficacy are realized when teachers work together on a team, such as a PLC+. When PLC+ teams collaborate toward shared goals and are successful with their efforts, their sense of collective teacher efficacy develops and the chances for feeling the runner's high, the collective flow, are increased.

Collaboration is a driving force to develop collective teacher efficacy; one cannot do it alone. When PLC+ team members collaborate and attain shared goals, they become more motivated and their expectations for future success increase. This is collective teacher efficacy in action. There is a realization that the team can solve problems that an individual cannot.

Similarly, collective teacher efficacy provides the fuel teams need to maintain course when bumps or glitches are encountered. "As people's sense of efficacy grows stronger, they become more courageous and confident in dealing with difficult circumstances, recasting them in ways that appear more manageable" (Evans, 2009, p. 70). Since teaching is a highly emotional undertaking, it's clear that actively participating in collaborative processes that foster collective teacher efficacy to emerge will benefit educators and students alike.

VISION OF TEACHING AND LEARNING

Our vision is that every educator goes to work each day feeling inspired and confident to positively impact students' lives. Once they arrive at school, we hope that they

- Feel valued as professionals

- Are engaged in high-performing teams as part of their regular workdays

- Experience that high levels of trust, care, and collaboration are cultural norms at the school

- Routinely confer with colleagues to examine their practices

- Willingly accept collective responsibility for student learning, even for students who are not in their classrooms

These qualities, though aspirational, are attainable in all of our schools. Just as runners train for races using the best know-how in the field, educators should also prepare using the best know-how in our field. This knowledge can be found in the Visible Learning® Meta^X, a highly respected research base that contains findings from studies related to student achievement from literally millions of students around the globe. From this vast research, we know that collective teacher efficacy has a 1.36 effect size on student achievement, even "after controlling for previous student achievement and demographic characteristics such as socioeconomic status" (Klassen et al., 2010, p. 466). This is a significantly above-average influence (0.40) and one that should significantly accelerate student learning. Clearly, cultivating collective teacher efficacy should be a priority for all educators and policy makers.

Sharing lesson plans or meeting every Tuesday afternoon only gets teams so far. Collective teacher efficacy isn't developed because administrators expect educators to collaborate. Instead, collective teacher efficacy is ignited by collaborative processes, the pooling of resources and energy, and mutual accountability. Further, collective teacher efficacy can be developed systematically, yet flexibly. This playbook provides teams with the tools to implement evidence-based practices that hone their expertise as professional educators. In so doing, teams produce and harness the energy that propels learning forward. And when teachers learn, so do students.

When teachers learn, so do students.

The pathway we offer defines how teams can systematically cultivate and increase motivation and energy as individuals and, importantly, with each other. We show how each component of a Collective Efficacy Cycle can be ideally implemented, which provides educators with an understanding of what the desired destination looks like. This approach closely aligns with the PLC+ framework, in which educators are provided with practical strategies and tools to engage in collaborative learning experiences that focus on the following five questions.

PLC+ Framework Guiding Questions

1. **Where are we going?**
2. **Where are we now?**
3. **How do we move learning forward?**
4. **What did we learn today?**
5. **Who benefited and who did not benefit?**

This playbook highlights the value of question 4: *What did we learn today?* While promoting student learning and well-being is our shared purpose, this playbook focuses on *adults'* ongoing learning and deepening expertise as professional educators. In schools where there isn't a shared commitment to adult learning, teachers often "turn inward, relying only on their own experience" (Bird & Little, 1986, p. 495). Research indicates that teaching is not a static profession; rather, effective instruction "requires a solid and continuing education for educators" (Joyce & Calhoun, 2015, p. 43).

HOW A COLLECTIVE EFFICACY CYCLE FITS WITHIN THE PLC+ FRAMEWORK

The Collective Efficacy Cycle is designed to correspond to the five PLC+ questions; teams use their existing knowledge to focus on addressing a common challenge. There is no need for existing PLC+ teams to learn a different structure. For teachers new to the PLC+ process, each of the five guiding questions is detailed in *PLC+: Better Decisions and Greater Impact by Design* (Fisher et al., 2020). The Collective Efficacy Cycle described in this book offers teacher teams an established process that can be used repeatedly; the content changes, but the process doesn't.

Figure 0.1 draws connections between the five PLC+ guiding questions and the Collective Efficacy Cycle.

FIGURE 0.1 CROSSWALK BETWEEN THE PLC+ FRAMEWORK AND THE COLLECTIVE EFFICACY CYCLE

PLC+ FRAMEWORK	COLLECTIVE EFFICACY CYCLE
Question 1: Where are we going?	• Forming a PLC+ team • Co-developing a Collective Efficacy Cycle
Question 2: Where are we now?	• Using formative information to determine student needs • Identifying the common challenge
Question 3: How do we move learning forward?	• Selecting an evidence-based strategy • Learning about the strategy
Question 4: What did we learn today?	• Implementing the strategy • Opening up practice through peer observations • Providing peer-to-peer feedback • Coaching colleagues • Reflecting on results
Question 5: Who benefited and who did not benefit?	• Making adjustments that lead to improved student outcomes • Validations and celebrations

The Collective Efficacy Cycle offers a way for teachers and schools to shift from isolated professional development events to creating cultures where professional learning is expected, received, and valued. While there have been many advances in the field of education, including the meta-analyses that determined 322 influences on student learning (Hattie, 2021), many innovative practices have not yet found their way to classrooms. Often, schools use professional development strategies and plans that have grown stale. This is unfortunate for both students and teachers, as students may be missing out on high-quality instruction and teachers may be missing out on professional learning experiences that could be energizing to their careers.

Additionally, it's important that all educators, including those who write educational policy, recognize the importance and value of teacher leadership. If teachers are left out of the school improvement equation and are solely relegated to their class-rooms with a set of directions to follow, many student achievement goals may not be realized. We will continue to fail too many of our students. Since teaching and learning are dynamic, it's essential that teachers are highly involved in all aspects of strengthening schools: strategic planning using evidence-based practices, imple-mentation, and assessment of student learning.

A VISUAL SCHEDULE

The Collective Efficacy Cycle is conceptualized through a visual schedule that provides a road map of the cycle and serves to keep oriented to the common challenge.

An example of a Collective Efficacy Cycle in fourth-grade mathematics is presented in Figure 0.2. Note that each square in the schedule isn't completed; it's not neces-sary, or possible, for teams to complete every square. Instead, use the schedule as a map to provide structure for the cycle. Teams are encour-aged to begin with a blank visual schedule and display it publicly. This supports team accountability but also signals to the school community what the team is learning about. Oth-ers will be interested in the cycle, which promotes another opportunity for collective efficacy to develop.

◄ **TONI EXPLAINS HOW THE VISUAL SCHEDULE IS USED**
resources.corwin.com/collectiveefficacy

NOTES

_____
_____
_____
_____
_____
_____
_____
_____
_____
_____
_____
_____
_____
_____
_____
_____

FIGURE 0.2 COLLECTIVE EFFICACY CYCLE VISUAL SCHEDULE EXAMPLE

Common Challenge: Relying on algorithms/tools to solve math problems

Evidence-Based Strategy: Student-led questioning

CYCLE # 1 DATE SPAN:	COMMON CHALLENGE Dialogue about student learning needs	BUILDING KNOWLEDGE Professional learning for staff to implement an evidence-based practice	SAFE PRACTICE Educators experiment with the new practice in a low-risk environment	PROFESSIONAL READING Teachers receive professional articles relevant to the practice being learned	OPENING UP PRACTICE Educators observe each other and engage in structured reflections and feedback	MONITORING, MODIFYING, AND CELEBRATING Educators engage in learning walks during and after school to discuss student learning	NEXT STEPS Teachers review evidence of student learning and determine next steps
Week 1: 9/7	Dialogue						
Week 2: 9/14		9/14 telling vs. facilitating		9/14–9/25 Chapter 2, *Number Talks*, pp. 38–54			
Week 3: 9/21		9/21 making S's thinking public	9/21–9/25				9/21 sentence starters, chart
Week 4: 9/28	Dialogue	9/28 small group number talks, scaffolds	9/28–10/2	9/28–10/2 Chapter 2, *Number Talks*, pp. 55–59			

(Continued)

FIGURE 0.2 (CONTINUED)

Common Challenge: Relying on algorithms/tools to solve math problems

Evidence-Based Strategy: Student-led questioning

CYCLE # 1 DATE SPAN:	COMMON CHALLENGE Dialogue about student learning needs	BUILDING KNOWLEDGE Professional learning for staff to implement an evidence-based practice	SAFE PRACTICE Educators experiment with the new practice in a low-risk environment	PROFESSIONAL READING Teachers receive professional articles relevant to the practice being learned	OPENING UP PRACTICE Educators observe each other and engage in structured reflections and feedback	MONITORING, MODIFYING, AND CELEBRATING Educators engage in learning walks during and after school to discuss student learning	NEXT STEPS Teachers review evidence of student learning and determine next steps
Week 5: 10/5		10/25 small group number talks, scaffolds	10/5–10/9				
Week 6: 10/12					10/12–10/16 triad obs.	10/16 ghost visit: chart	
Week 7: 10/19	Dialogue				10/19–10/2 triad obs.	10/23 guided visit: chart, questioning	10/19 review recordings
Week 8: 10/26	Dialogue						10/26 review recordings

Source: Adapted from Chula Vista Elementary School District, 2018.

While collaborative learning experiences foster teachers' continuing education, there are three specific actions teams must take to set up opportunities to generate collective teacher efficacy:

- Learning evidence-based practices to implement with students
- Determining and attaining a shared goal
- Opening up practice through peer-to-peer observations

After all, collective teacher efficacy isn't possible if you're unaware of your colleagues' practices. These are three specific fundamental actions that generate collective teacher efficacy.

Three Specific, Fundamental Actions That Generate Collective Teacher Efficacy

1. Implementing evidence-based practices with students
2. Determining and attaining a shared goal
3. Opening up practice through peer observations

COMPONENTS OF A COLLECTIVE EFFICACY CYCLE

The six modules in this playbook are organized to facilitate teams through a complete Collective Efficacy Cycle, which typically lasts for six to 10 weeks. A cycle is organized around a common challenge that can be addressed by implementing an evidence-based instructional strategy. These may include reciprocal teaching, jigsaw, close reading, or any other strategy that has been shown to accelerate student learning.

It takes time to learn about and implement an evidence-based strategy effectively. One-and-done professional development sessions aren't sufficient for us to gain the knowledge and skills to use a new strategy with students. Research tells us that we need to practice "with peers and small groups of students from 10 to 15 times before a high level of skill becomes evident" (Joyce & Showers, 1982, p. 6). Given that a cycle is structured for about two months, the timeline provides educators multiple opportunities to learn deeply about one strategy. Over the course of the cycle, the expectation is that educators collaboratively

- Use data to determine the area of student need
- Identify an evidence-based strategy that addresses the need
- Read about and discuss the strategy with the team
- Implement and practice the strategy multiple times with students

- Observe others and be observed while implementing the strategy
- Make necessary adjustments to promote student success
- Validate and celebrate success

While the cycle repeats throughout each school year and is flexible, we recommend that teams follow the modules in order until you're comfortable with the process. We also encourage equity of voice in your team so that each member has opportunities to be the team's activator throughout a cycle. The activator is a member of the team who has the skills required to engage peers in conversations and learning.

A cycle is guided by the data, not by external mandates.

The focus of a cycle is determined by the student achievement or well-being data that is presented and examined by the PLC+ team. A cycle is guided by the data, not by external mandates. This is an important aspect of the Collective Efficacy Cycle. In addition to deepening ownership by selecting the evidence-based strategy to address student needs, educators' agency is promoted because they make this determination. This provides flexibility for each team to select a focus that is relevant to their students' needs. We also encourage teams to invite other educators, such as school counselors and classroom assistants, to participate in a cycle.

HOW THE PLAYBOOK WORKS

Module 1 defines what self-efficacy and collective efficacy are so you develop an understanding of the science behind these concepts. We explain four ways teams systematically cultivate collective efficacy in their schools. To illustrate how this looks in action, we contrast a team with a low level of collective efficacy to one with a high level of collective efficacy. Tools are provided to assess the degree of individual and team efficacy in your contexts and determine next steps. Components and descriptions of the Collective Efficacy Cycle are provided in Figure 0.3.

The subsequent modules open with an Innovation Configuration (IC) map that defines the expectations for the team's success, as opposed to an individual's (Hall & Hord, 2015). Though similar to a rubric, an IC map provides teams with the specific behaviors and dispositions that are expected of each team member, because collective teacher efficacy isn't developed alone. Just like our students, when we understand the goal and criteria for success, we're more likely to be successful.

Module 2 supports teams to use data to determine a common challenge, which centers on students' needs. This is the focus of the Collective Efficacy Cycle. Teams who co-determine a common challenge establish the first of the three fundamental actions that generate collective teacher efficacy.

In Module 3, the team identifies evidence-based practices that will address the identified area of students' needs. From these possibilities, teams select one strategy to learn about. This may include reading about the strategy in an article, a module from a book, or perhaps in a blog. Or it may involve more formalized professional learning experiences. There can be think-alouds, modeling, and discussion of the strategy during team meetings so members gain a deep understanding of it. Setting a goal by committing to learning about an evidence- based strategy is the second of the three fundamental actions that lead to collective teacher efficacy.

While our team is learning about the evidence-based strategy, we also implement it with students. This is the subject of Module 4: Collaborative Planning and Safe Practice. During Safe Practice, we try out the strategy multiple times. We become more comfortable and skilled each time. The Safe Practice phase protects us from being observed or evaluated. We can feel safe to make adjustments if the lesson isn't promoting student learning to the degree they would like. Without this phase, implementation is less likely to occur as we all use our tried-and-true approaches when we know we are going to be observed. After all, we don't want to open ourselves up to criticism as we are learning a new technique. During this phase, we confer with each other about their implementation of the strategy and students' progress.

After a few weeks of safe practice, peer-to-peer observations are scheduled. The tools and protocols in Module 5 support teams to open up practice by observing each other's classrooms in non-evaluative ways. These observations, while usually 10 to 15 minutes in length, are the hallmark of the Collective Efficacy Cycle. Through observations, you will deepen your understanding of the evidence-based strategy and have opportunities to coach others and be coached. Peer-to-peer mentorship provides powerful learning experiences for both the mentor and the mentee, and the ability to mentor another educator isn't tied to a job title or years of experience. Rather, we guide you through the observation process, providing sample questions that help you to determine the impact on student learning. Peers observing each other is the third of the three actions necessary for collective teacher efficacy to develop during a Collective Efficacy Cycle.

> **Validation is both healthy and necessary for educators to flourish, individually and as team members.**

After weeks of learning about evidence-based practice, teams monitor student learning and make any necessary adjustments to ensure students are successful. This is the focus of Module 6. Assessment data is collected and evaluated so you can respond to student needs immediately. At the end of a Collective Efficacy Cycle, it's important that our team pause and collectively assess our impact on student learning, but also on our own learning.

◄ TAKING STOCK AND RECOGNIZING TEAM EFFORTS REGULARLY
resources.corwin.com/collectiveefficacy

In Module 6, we also celebrate the success of our team and share our learnings with the school through a gallery walk or another protocol that allows learning and innovation to spread. Witnessing others' learnings through a gallery walk prompts vicarious experiences, a precursor to collective efficacy, for others in the school. In educational settings, there is often an inherent, yet unspoken norm to be humble and modest about one's accomplishments. We assert that validation is both healthy and necessary for educators to flourish, individually and as team members. The tools and protocols included in this module help your team to systematically process, acknowledge, and celebrate students' learning, as well as your own. At the end of a cycle, there is closure and teams take stock of their sense of collective efficacy and determine their next steps.

FIGURE 0.3   COLLECTIVE EFFICACY CYCLE COMPONENTS AND DESCRIPTIONS

MODULE	COLLECTIVE EFFICACY CYCLE COMPONENTS	DESCRIPTION	MAJOR TOPICS AND TOOLS
1	Developing Individual and Collective Efficacy	Self and collective efficacy are defined. The four conditions for creating collective teacher efficacy are described.	• Self-efficacy self-assessment • Seven norms of collaborative work • Seeking mastery and vicarious experiences • Assessing and strengthening team efficacy, flexibility, craftsmanship, consciousness, and interdependence • Mindful moments
2	Determining the Common Challenge	A guided process for teams to use data to identify student learning needs. Teams develop a shared goal to address one need during the Collective Efficacy Cycle.	• Data collection and analysis protocols • Common challenge checklist and tuning protocol • Mindful moments
3	Building Educator Knowledge and Skills	Teams select learning opportunities to build knowledge and enhance professional skills about one evidence-based practice.	• Databases to find evidence-based practices • Learning log • Seven design elements of professional learning and pitfalls to avoid • Appealing to the head, heart, and hands when learning something new • Professional readings • Discussion and text-based protocols • Modeling and think-aloud planning tool • Mindful moments

MODULE	COLLECTIVE EFFICACY CYCLE COMPONENTS	DESCRIPTION	MAJOR TOPICS AND TOOLS
4	Collaborative Planning and Safe Practice	Team members engage in deliberate practice in their classrooms to deepen their expertise about the identified evidence-based practice.	• Naïve vs. deliberate practice • Reflective questions about deliberate practice • Reframing judgmental thoughts • The Ladder of Inference • Educator agency • Mindful moments
5	Collaborative Planning and Opening Up Practice	Team members observe the evidence-based practice being implemented in each other's classrooms for 15 minutes.	• Three components of peer-to-peer observations • Preparing for learning walks and ghost walks • Debriefing learning walks and ghost walks • Microteaching • Formal coaching • Cognitive coaching
6	Monitoring, Modifying, and Celebrating	As a result of the evidence-based practice, student learning is gauged. Teams reflect on their own learning and impact, which affirms their efforts.	• Success analysis protocol • Gallery walk facilitation guide • What collective efficacy sounds like • Tool to assess organizational readiness to scale • Individual and team assessment of the Collective Efficacy Cycle

(Continued)

FIGURE 0.3 (CONTINUED)

MODULE	COLLECTIVE EFFICACY CYCLE COMPONENTS	DESCRIPTION	MAJOR TOPICS AND TOOLS
	Appendices: Resources for Teams	Additional resources for individuals and teams to use to build trust, ensure successful meetings, and facilitate consensus. Tools to support teams to manage conflict and overcome barriers are provided.	• Collective Efficacy Cycle Visual Schedule Template • Innovation Configuration (IC) Map Action Planner • Trust on Our Team • Self-Assessment for Individual Contributions to Meetings • Successful Meetings Card Sort Activity • Benefits of Recording Notes Visibly and Publicly • Tips for Productive PLC+ Meetings • Conflict in Teams • Facilitating Consensus • Focusing Four Consensus Protocol • Group Dynamics in PLC+ Meetings

The playbook is designed to explicitly teach teacher teams how to systematically cultivate collective efficacy. We encourage you to write it in and keep it nearby throughout the cycle. There are numerous activities and structured reflections that will assist you in refining your teaching craft. Each is designed to invite you to record your individual thinking as well as thoughts generated collaboratively by your team. Please use the playbook to set goals, monitor, track progress, and ensure everyone on your team is on the same page. It's also a way for teams to document the steps taken throughout a cycle, which may be useful for future team efforts or other operational processes at the school.

The playbook also invites teams to examine their own understandings and assumptions as individuals, because people interpret professional learning experiences in different ways. These are opportunities for individuals to learn about each other at deeper levels, and in so doing, become more calibrated and connected as a team. By engaging in these activities and committing to action, we're confident this process will provide teams with the means to understand, develop, and sustain collective efficacy in your schools. We're optimistic this process will affirm and energize you.

 Access videos and resources for the introduction at
resources.corwin.com/collectiveefficacy

NOTES

NOTES

Module 1
DEVELOPING INDIVIDUAL AND COLLECTIVE EFFICACY

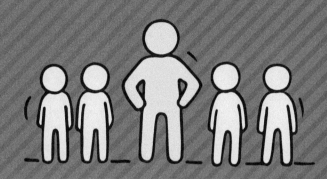

MODULE OVERVIEW

Collective efficacy doesn't just happen. It occurs when particular conditions are established by teams who believe that a group of people can solve problems that an individual cannot. When PLC+ teams collaborate and accomplish shared goals, they feel empowered and their sense of collective teacher efficacy increases.

In this module, we define what individual and collective efficacy mean. We explain four ways teams can systematically cultivate collective efficacy in their schools:

- Mastery experiences
- Vicarious experiences
- Social persuasion
- Positive emotional states

INTRODUCTION TO MODULE 1
resources.corwin.com/collectiveefficacy

ACT 1: WORK HARDER, NOT SMARTER

Fourth-grade teacher Dina arrives at school on a Tuesday morning. After dropping off her teaching bag in her classroom, she pulls a blackline master that reteaches students how to determine cause-and-effect. Dina takes the worksheet to the copy room where she runs into her colleague, Julia, who also teaches fourth grade. The two teachers exchange pleasantries, and Julia asks what Dina is teaching today. Dina explains that most of her students understood the lesson (cause-and-effect) yesterday, but there are always "those same five kids that just don't get it. I'm going to have them work on this." She points to the remedial worksheet. Julia looks and agrees. "Yeah, it's the same in my class. But look what I found. I downloaded this for cause-and-effect so my struggling readers can have more practice. Do you want a copy?"

Meanwhile, Tracy, who is sitting nearby, listens but does not interject. She thinks to herself, *Yeah, but it's still a worksheet. Of course, I have students who need additional instruction, but I think that meeting with them in a small group and teaching it with new material is a better plan. I think I might even gamify it and have students work together to figure out the effects based on causes.*

Many teachers like Dina, Julia, and Tracy work in isolation. They arrive at school each morning, head to their classrooms, and close their doors. When they collaborate, it's usually about a common formative assessment that they all must give. There often isn't discussion about scaffolds and supports for learners, nor is there talk about the effectiveness of their lessons. Teachers follow prescribed pacing guides and programs, at times without thoughtful planning or reflection on student learning. Going through the motions year after year may even diminish the passion many felt during their first years of teaching.

Dina, Julia, and Tracy aren't bad teachers. They care about their kids and believe they hold high expectations for student learning. They receive strong evaluations from their administrators, so there's no compelling reason to do anything different from year to year. They may not know of other ways to teach. They may be unaware that their collaboration could look and feel different. Use Figure 1.1 to note your thoughts, and at the end of this module, we'll revisit this scenario to see how collaboration between Dina, Julia, and Tracy could look.

FIGURE 1.1 A MINDFUL MOMENT

Have you ever been a part of a school-based group that didn't really have an instructional purpose? If so, what was the context? How did it feel when you met with this group? What might have made it better?

WHAT IS EFFICACY?

Would you purchase a car that doesn't pass safety tests? Should a doctor prescribe a medication that hasn't been shown to effectively treat a disease? In healthcare and other fields, it's a common practice that treatments and products undergo research and testing in order to validate claims about their efficacy. Efficacy is a measure of a desired effect. Consumers can research the efficacy of the products they purchase and the medications they take. Measures of efficacy are also studied in education. In addition to testing strategies and interventions, educational researchers study and measure teachers' efficacy, because efficacy is related to effort. In this way, we can think about efficacy and effort as a teacher's capacity to produce a desired effect, such as an effect on student learning.

Achievement is more complex and greater than the sum of teachers' individual contributions.

In the 1990s, Stanford University psychologist Albert Bandura identified that students' academic achievement in schools is reflective of the efforts of a collective group, meaning that achievement is more complex and greater than the sum of teachers' individual contributions. Bandura found that teachers who work together may develop a strong sense of collective efficacy within their school community. These combined efforts contribute significantly to students' academic achievement (Bandura, 1997).

Academic success is usually measured by student achievement levels, and all schools and districts are charged with improving student learning. Within a school, the organizational structure is influenced by the relationships between students, teachers, and administrators. According to social cognitive theory, teachers' perceptions of themselves and their colleagues affect their actions. Bandura (2000) recognized that collective efficacy develops when a group perseveres toward shared goals, takes risks together, and has a desire to stay together. The willingness to stay together marks a professional commitment because "people do not live their lives in individual autonomy. Indeed, many of the outcomes they seek are achievable only through interdependent efforts. Hence, they have to work together to secure what they cannot accomplish on their own" (p. 75).

Additionally, social cognitive theory suggests that individual and collective efficacy beliefs are influenced by the environment, other people, and personal factors. These beliefs impact how people think, act, feel, and motivate themselves. Through social processes in a school, efficacy beliefs form as individuals come to believe they can make a difference for students through their collective efforts (Bandura, 1997). Goddard and colleagues (2000) determined that collective teacher efficacy is a stronger predictor of student achievement than socioeconomic status and other school characteristics. Other studies report similar findings (Hattie, 2021; Klassen et al., 2010; Tschannen-Moran & Barr, 2004). Since collective efficacy is associated with student achievement, it's important to understand the differences between self-efficacy and collective efficacy.

SELF-EFFICACY

Self-efficacy is a person's belief in their own ability to take actions that lead to a specific result. It's the "conviction that one can successfully execute the behavior required to produce outcomes" (Bandura, 1977, p. 193). This belief, on the part of the individual, is that they can take the necessary actions such that a desired result is attained. Teacher self-efficacy is a teacher's belief that they are capable of taking the actions necessary to assure positive student learning outcomes.

Teacher self-efficacy refers to a "teacher's sense of competence—not some objective measure of actual competence" (Protheroe, 2008, p. 43). This sense of competence is context specific and forms as teachers assess their personal competence in relation to the given demands of a particular situation. For example, a teacher might feel capable of teaching early literacy but feel less capable when teaching mathematics at a conceptual level.

Bandura (2000) and others have shown that an individual's self-efficacy plays a major role in how a person approaches tasks, goals, and challenges. People with a strong sense of self-efficacy

- Develop deeper interest in activities
- Are more committed to self-identified goals
- Recover more quickly from setbacks and disappointments
- Understand that challenges are normal and take steps to overcome them

In contrast, people with a low sense of self-efficacy tend to

- Avoid challenging situations
- Believe that difficult tasks and situations are beyond their capabilities
- Focus on negative outcomes and personal shortcomings
- Lose confidence and give up

For a quick, informal assessment of your own self-efficacy levels at work, consider the questions in Figure 1.2 on the following page. Record your initial thoughts about your efficacy in terms of teaching and learning.

> Collective teacher efficacy is a stronger predictor of student achievement than socioeconomic status and other school characteristics.

NOTES

_____

_____

_____

_____

_____

_____

_____

_____

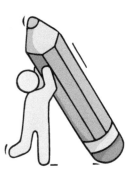

FIGURE 1.2 SELF-EFFICACY SELF-ASSESSMENT

QUESTIONS	THOUGHTS AND NOTES
Do you feel like you can handle problems that come your way? **YES** **NO**	
Are you confident in your ability to achieve your goals? **YES** **NO**	
Do you feel like you can manage unexpected events that come up? **YES** **NO**	
Are you able to bounce back fairly quickly after a stressful event? **YES** **NO**	
Can you manage yourself well when under pressure? **YES** **NO**	
Do you keep trying when things become difficult? **YES** **NO**	

Collaborating Through Collective Efficacy Cycles

If you answered *Yes* to many of the questions in the self-assessment, then chances are good that you have a fairly strong sense of self-efficacy. If you feel like your self-efficacy could use a boost, identify one of the statements in Figure 1.2 and a goal for yourself. Start with baby steps. You'll feel good when you accomplish the goal, so consider what is attainable so you can be successful. And remember, success breeds success.

COLLECTIVE EFFICACY

Similar to an individual's belief in his or her capabilities to ensure student achievement, collective teacher efficacy refers to a group's beliefs about their competence for successful student learning outcomes. Collective teacher efficacy, then, is an attitude shared by teachers: by working together, they can make a difference for students. This, too, is context specific because collective beliefs are shaped by teachers' perceptions about the staff's teaching competence, their perceptions of the challenges related to educating their students, as well as available supports to foster positive student outcomes (Goddard, 2001). Collective teacher efficacy is "associated with the tasks, level of effort, persistence, shared thoughts, stress levels, and achievement of groups" (Goddard et al., 2000, p. 482).

Schools are complex social organizations and the interactions between teachers, students, and administrators affect the culture of the organization. Culture develops and grows through an "accumulation of actions, traditions, symbols, ceremonies, and rituals" (Fisher et al., 2012, p. 6). Because of these interplays, people who work in a school may come to form and share certain perceptions. Collective teacher efficacy, then, develops based upon a staff's collective analysis of the teaching and learning environment and their assessment of their teaching competence (Pierce, 2019). This means that collective efficacy beliefs are malleable and can be shaped by intentional actions: mastery experiences, vicarious experiences, social persuasion, and affective states (Bandura, 1977). We'll explore each of these four sources of collective teacher efficacy in the following sections.

◄ FOUR SOURCES OF
COLLECTIVE EFFICACY
resources.corwin.com/collectiveefficacy

Collective Efficacy Source 1: Mastery Experiences

The most powerful source of collective teacher efficacy is acquired through mastery experiences. When teams experience success and attribute that success to dynamics within their control, their feelings of collective efficacy increase. With each success the team experiences, they come to believe and expect that they can repeat it. As they say, success breeds success.

The opposite is also true, as a series of failures tend to undermine a team's sense of efficacy. This can also be understood through the notion of the self-fulfilling prophecy. A self-fulfilling prophecy is when a belief or expectation about a future event comes true, even when we aren't consciously aware that we hold that expectation. In simpler terms, it's a prediction that comes true because our beliefs and expectations have influenced our behavior at a subconscious level. Stereotype threat and the Placebo Effect are both examples of self-fulfilling prophecies.

We can see that self-fulfilling prophecies influence our thoughts and behavior—both good and bad. When we believe something about ourselves, we are more likely to act in ways that align with our beliefs, thus confirming our beliefs and encouraging the same behavior. Similarly, when we believe something about others, we may act in ways that reinforce those assumptions.

Self-fulfilling prophecies influence our thoughts and behavior—both good and bad.

It's important that teams are aware of their beliefs and the nature of their interactions. Do people use asset-oriented language when describing students or is the talk more deficit-based? To reduce cycles of negative thinking and behavior, we need to pay attention to our assumptions and interactions we have about our assumptions. For instance, a teacher who voices a statement such as "Those kids can't learn" or "They just don't care" sends messages to other educators that may be easily transferred into reality. Whether we're aware of it or not, our beliefs and expectations influence ourselves, but also seep into communications with others. As Henry Ford famously said, "Whether you think you can or think you can't, you're right."

Since negative talk can alter reality, it's important that teams are aware of their communication patterns and commit to monitoring them. In so doing, the team increases the likelihood that mastery experiences will occur. Mastery experiences include developing shared goals and collaboratively engaging in learning activities. As teams experience successes, their momentum continues and their confidence and resiliency as a collective also increase. Mastery experiences are often cultivated when teachers work together in PLC+ teams.

Communication and Conditions
That Build Mastery Experiences

We shouldn't assume that adults know how to work together effectively because they are part of a team. Teachers that are mandated to work together as a team, such as departments and grade levels, may feel these relationships are contrived by administrators. They may perceive a lack of emotional depth from team members. Teachers need to feel supported because of the "pervasively emotional nature of teaching" (Horn & Little, 2010, p. 197).

By paying attention to how we interact during collegial interactions, closer working relationships can be fostered, and the chances of participating in a mastery experience increase. However, if teams are reluctant to share ideas or beliefs, there is little hope for mastery experiences, and consequentially, collective teacher efficacy, to emerge.

To systematically structure meetings that cultivate mastery experiences, wise teams gain an awareness of their current communication styles and determine improvements that support the team's functioning. Since tensions mount when groups communicate ineffectively, a self-review at regular intervals can prevent issues before they fester. Garmston and Wellman (1999) recommend seven norms of collaborative work to guide team interactions:

1. Pausing

2. Paraphrasing

3. Probing for specificity

4. Putting ideas on the table

5. Paying attention to self and others

6. Presuming positive intentions

7. Pursuing a balance between advocacy and inquiry

These are skills that anyone can use to improve communication in meetings and during interactions with others. These norms are deceptively simple, and most are skills that most people have. Garmston and Wellman (1999) say this is ironic because

> these seemingly simple behaviors are rare in many meetings. Pausing and paraphrasing are often missing, especially when things get tense. Probing for details is forgotten when members presume to understand others' meanings. This can lead to later confusion and complication. Presuming positive intentions prevents members from judging others. Interpersonal judgments spawn blocked thinking and negative presuppositions. Advocating and inquiring into the ideas of others increases the capacity for group members to influence each other. (p. 38)

Taking time and care to establish shared meeting norms is worth the effort. Doing so enhances the team's communication skills, promoting team members to interact in ways that cause mastery experiences to occur. When these norms of collaborative work become an established part of how your team operates, the cohesion, energy, and commitment to shared goals increase dramatically. The team's sense of collective efficacy grows.

Reflect on your current interpersonal and intrapersonal communication skills. Note these in Figure 1.3 and consider ways you might strengthen them to improve future relationships.

NOTES

_____

_____

_____

_____

_____

_____

_____

FIGURE 1.3 INDEPENDENT REFLECTION FOR PERSONAL COMMUNICATION GROWTH

SEVEN NORMS OF COLLABORATIVE WORK	MY CURRENT SKILLS	WAYS TO STRENGTHEN
Pausing		
Paraphrasing		
Probing questions		
Putting ideas on the table		
Paying attention to self and others		
Presuming positive intentions		
Pursuing advocacy/inquiry		

Source: Adapted from Garmston and Wellman (1999).

Now, select one of the seven norms of collaborative work you would like to polish by noting it in Figure 1.4. Consider sharing this goal with your team members so they can support your efforts.

FIGURE 1.4   IMPROVING MY COMMUNICATION

Norm to improve:	
How will this improve your personal relationships?	
How will it improve your professional relationships?	
How will you know you're successful?	

Collective Efficacy Source 2:
Vicarious Experiences

The second source of collective efficacy is realized through vicarious experiences. Vicarious experiences are situations that are witnessed by others; they aren't directly involved in the situation, but they see and feel it. Bandura (1977) asserts that observing others similar to oneself succeed prompts observers to believe that they too possess the capabilities to master comparable activities. Essentially, vicarious experiences are modeling events in which we see someone else succeed in the face of a challenge. Watching someone else achieve a goal gives us the confidence that we can too.

Modeling comes from a wide range of sources, including colleagues, coaches, mentors, and many others. Importantly, individuals are not "dependent on direct experience" (Manz & Sims, 1981, p. 106) for learning to take place. Modeling provides more than a social standard by which one can judge their own capability. Through their behavior and by thinking out loud, skilled models transmit knowledge and teach others how to approach and overcome challenges. Models inspire and motivate, and, importantly, increase others' self-efficacy.

Increasing self-efficacy can have profound effects on the way others think, act, and relate to one another. When teachers see their colleagues face similar challenges, and fare successfully, there are expectations that they too can overcome obstacles or setbacks. It's important that teams discuss these moments so that meaning of the event is processed together. In this way, teams can cultivate collective efficacy through vicarious experiences.

Teams can initiate vicarious experiences by observing others in their own school, by observing teachers or teams in other schools like their own, and through video observations. It's important that teams debrief these situations and not make assumptions that each team member interpreted events in the same way. It's helpful to dialogue about these events in structured ways.

Using Figure 1.5, collaborate with your team to brainstorm about individuals (or teams) that you've heard good things about. Perhaps students have mentioned how riveted they feel when in a certain biology teacher's classroom. Maybe you've heard students rave about how much they loved their third-grade teacher because "she made learning sooo fun." Who are these models? What opportunities might there be to learn from colleagues in your building or at a school nearby? When discussing and noting these ideas, the team may realize there's an abundance of expertise they can access, which initiates vicarious experiences.

FIGURE 1.5 INITIATING VICARIOUS EXPERIENCES

PEOPLE IN OUR SCHOOL	PEOPLE WE KNOW IN OTHER SCHOOLS	OPPORTUNITIES USING VIDEO

Collective Efficacy Source 3: Social Persuasion

A third way that teams can generate collective efficacy is through social persuasion. When you think about persuasion, what comes to mind? You might think of advertising messages that compel consumers to purchase a particular product, while others might think about a political candidate who tries to sway voters in their favor. Persuasion is a powerful force in our everyday lives.

When we think of persuasion, negative examples may be among the first that come to mind, but persuasion can also be used as a positive force. Social persuasion is a form of influence in which someone is encouraged to adopt an idea, attitude, or course of action. Goddard et al. (2000) maintain that people can be persuaded to believe they have the necessary skills and capabilities to succeed.

Persuasion is the ability to use your influence to cause someone to change their beliefs, ideas, or actions because of your reasoning or the information that you have presented. It's a voluntary choice, not manipulation, when persuasion techniques are used with integrity and a sincere intention to make a positive difference in a person's life or to the betterment of the group. Persuasion can be a lever for moving a group's decision process forward.

Cialdini (2007) suggests that people who have strong persuasion skills are those with strong communication skills and emotional intelligence. These qualities include

- Keeping promises
- Being reliable
- Taking responsibility
- Being sincere, genuine, and honest

Consider a time when someone gave you encouragement that helped you to accomplish a goal, and record it in Figure 1.6. Getting a verbal affirmation from a mentor or other respected individual often helps people to overcome self-doubt. With added encouragement, people may give extra effort to the task at hand.

> **People can be persuaded to believe they have the necessary skills and capabilities to succeed.**

NOTES

_____

_____

_____

_____

_____

_____

_____

_____

FIGURE 1.6   SOCIAL PERSUASION

Someone who taught or mentored me:	**Someone I will teach or mentor:**
Someone who supported or helped me:	**Someone I will support or help:**
Someone who encouraged me:	**Someone I will encourage:**

Collective Efficacy Source 4: Positive Emotional States

The fourth source of collective efficacy involves the affective conditions at the school. Sometimes referred to as the "emotional tone of the organization" (Tschannen-Moran & Barr, 2004, p. 6), the affective conditions include the school's culture, as well as an individual's feelings of excitement or anxiety. Attention to the school's culture is significant, as people may construe and internalize feelings of competence, or inadequacy, based upon the mood of the school.

Positive school culture attracts talent, elevates happiness and satisfaction, drives engagement, and affects people's performance. It can reinforce educators' trust in one another and provide an environment that's psychologically safe. Reflect independently in the second column in Figure 1.7 about your school's culture. What have you noticed about the mood and tone? What does this mean for the well-being and functioning of your team? Your team might consider setting aside time to explore your collective thoughts so you have a more nuanced perspective. Notes jotted in the third column may help your team to determine appropriate next steps.

FIGURE 1.7 SCHOOL CULTURE REFLECTION

SCHOOL CULTURE	MY REFLECTIONS	OUR COLLECTIVE THOUGHTS
What do I notice about the school culture? What dynamics and vibes are present?		
How do I feel about the school's culture?		
What do I want our school culture to sound and feel like? What defines a positive school culture for me?		
What am I willing to do for our team's health?		
What does this mean for our team?		
What's a first step I can take?		

As teams use the information learned about the school culture through the individual and team reflections in Figure 1.7, what implications bubble up? Does the information shared compel you to take action? For example, if the team discovers there's a shared concern about students' behavior during passing periods, perhaps team members could commit to some hallway TLC by being more visible between classes and initiating positive interactions with students a few times each week. Small actions add up and everyone benefits from an enhanced school culture.

They say that life is 10% what happens to you and 90% is how you react to it. We all do better work when we experience that what we do matters, that it is valuable, and that our presence makes a difference to others. We may know in our hearts that what we do matters, but it is certainly confirming to hear these affirmations from others. We do not, after all, work and live in a vacuum.

Since teaching is a highly personal vocation, without planned interactions around a common focus, we risk that people might feel isolated from the other adults in the school. Instead, we can intentionally design a work environment where people bond over shared aspirations, feel valued for their uniqueness, and have a voice in the decisions that affect them. In order for people to know each other really well, we need to tell specifically how and when we feel valued. Others may not be aware of our specific "love language," so sharing this with others increases the cohesion between teams. Use Figure 1.8 to explore the value of being valued.

FIGURE 1.8 A MINDFUL MOMENT

Use the space below to identify three experiences when you felt valued at work. Describe the circumstances and outcomes for each experience and select one to share aloud with your team.

1.

2.

3.

Collective teacher efficacy can be cultivated systematically through mastery experiences, vicarious experiences, social persuasion, and positive emotional states. It doesn't just happen because teachers in a building gather together once a week. Instead, wise teams try to actively construct the conditions for collective efficacy to come about. They pay attention and are on the lookout for mastery experiences that forward learning. It is during these times the team is priming itself for the runner's high. This can be amplified when a positive school culture boosts their synergy.

FUELING HIGH-PERFORMING TEAMS

In addition to positive school culture, high-performing teams are fueled by five energy sources (Garmston & Wellman, 1999). Building up these reserves allows groups to increase their efficacy and efficiency, paving the way for enhanced learning and the time to practice and refine skills. These energy sources are

- Group efficacy
- Group flexibility
- Group craftmanship
- Group consciousness
- Group interdependence

MAINTAINING TEAM ENERGY
resources.corwin.com/collectiveefficacy

Use Figures 1.9 through 1.13 to assess the current state of your team in relation to each of the five energy sources. Reflect and note examples that support or limit your team's functioning. Consider the implications and indicate how your team might attend to one or more components.

NOTES

_____

_____

_____

_____

_____

_____

_____

_____

_____

_____

_____

_____

FIGURE 1.9 COMPONENTS OF GROUP EFFICACY

MY TEAM . . .	EXAMPLE/EVIDENCE	OPPORTUNITIES TO STRENGTHEN
Is motivated by and committed to accomplishing shared goals		
Productively manages the tension between the vision and current reality		
Focuses its resources to have the greatest impact		
Learns from experiences and doesn't repeat mistakes		

Source: Adapted from Garmston and Wellman (1999).

FIGURE 1.10 COMPONENTS OF GROUP FLEXIBILITY

MY TEAM . . .	EXAMPLE/EVIDENCE	OPPORTUNITIES TO STRENGTHEN
Honors and capitalizes on the diversity of the group		
Collectively shares perspectives and shifts when necessary		
Accesses multiple thinking and process skills		
Tends to rational and intuitive ways of working together		
Generates and considers multiple options to move forward		
Addresses internal stresses when they arise		

Source: Adapted from Garmston and Wellman (1999).

FIGURE 1.11 COMPONENTS OF GROUP CRAFTMANSHIP

MY TEAM . . .	EXAMPLE/EVIDENCE	OPPORTUNITIES TO STRENGTHEN
Creates, calibrates, and refines expectations of themselves		
Manages time effectively		
Invests energy on honing and investing process tools		
Honors pathways from novice to expert performance		
Continuously reviews and refines inter- and intra-group communications		

Source: Adapted from Garmston and Wellman (1999).

FIGURE 1.12 COMPONENTS OF GROUP CONSCIOUSNESS

MY TEAM . . .	EXAMPLE/EVIDENCE	OPPORTUNITIES TO STRENGTHEN
Is aware when assumptions and experience are interfering with learning		
Shares core values, norms, and a group identity		
Monitors progress toward meeting group expectations		
Has set criteria for decision making		
Objectively reflects on its processes and products regularly		

Source: Adapted from Garmston and Wellman (1999).

FIGURE 1.13 COMPONENTS OF GROUP INTERDEPENDENCE

MY TEAM . . .	EXAMPLE/EVIDENCE	OPPORTUNITIES TO STRENGTHEN
Envisions the potential of the group		
Values its interactions and trusts the processes of dialogue		
Optimizes its relationships and interconnections		
Regards disagreement and conflict as sources of learning and transformation for the group		

Source: Adapted from Garmston and Wellman (1999).

Since a group's energy is "influenced by cultural factors and the social context, which in turn reflect experience and learning" (Immordino-Yang, 2016, p. 87), wise teams pay attention to these interactions. A team's functioning also operates within the larger context of the school, which can promote or hinder growth. School culture is shaped and is "heavily dependent on the belief system of the staff of that school" (Kurz & Knight, 2003, p. 113).

The Collective Efficacy Cycle described in the upcoming modules uplifts teachers and defines a pathway for PLC+ teams to systematically cultivate collective efficacy.

In the next section, let's revisit the vignette that opened this module. In this revised view, collective efficacy fuels the fourth-grade team.

NOTES

_____

_____

_____

_____

_____

_____

_____

_____

_____

_____

_____

_____

_____

_____

_____

_____

_____

_____

_____

_____

_____

_____

ACT 2: WORK SMARTER, NOT HARDER

Fourth-grade teacher Dina arrives at school on a Tuesday morning. After dropping off her teaching bag in her classroom, she heads to fellow fourth-grade teacher Julia's classroom. Dina is concerned because many students in her classroom didn't respond well to her lesson on cause-and-effect yesterday. She knows this because she collected formative assessments on exit tickets, as did the other fourth-grade teachers. After reviewing the exit tickets after school, Dina texted Julia and Tracy to ask if they could meet the following morning to compare data from each class. The team agreed and decided to meet in Julia's room the following morning.

During this 15-minute meeting, the three teachers collaboratively analyze the exit ticket data and realize that 22 of 25 students in Tracy's class had understood cause-and-effect yesterday. Dina and Julia ask if Tracy would be willing to share how she had provided this instruction to her students. "Oh, yes, absolutely," Tracy replies. "Let me show you how I set up my small group instruction and collaborative groups yesterday. . . ."

In this enhanced version of the experience, there isn't a competition between Dina, Julia, and Tracy. Instead, there's a focus on student learning because this team utilizes formative information to determine their teaching effectiveness and how to adjust to ensure students are successful. As a result of this collaboration, the team's thinking and actions become more closely linked together (Hattie & Zierer, 2018). This willingness to discuss student learning and learn together leads to collective teacher efficacy.

MODULE 1 RECAP: WHAT DID WE LEARN?

Yay, team! You've reached the end of the first module and we hope that you agree that teamwork makes the dream work. Instead of waiting and hoping feelings of collective efficacy will appear, teams can work smarter by actively creating the conditions to foster it. Contributing to a mastery experience or being exposed to one vicariously can be energizing and bring the team closer together. Teams who work smarter also uplift one another. They pay attention to their social context and proactively nurture positive emotions that deepen relational trust.

 Access videos and resources for this module at
resources.corwin.com/collectiveefficacy

NOTES

Module 2
DETERMINING THE COMMON CHALLENGE

MODULE OVERVIEW

Teacher teams are encouraged to work together toward a shared goal or common challenge so that they have a collective purpose. The common challenge is determined internally by your team as you examine student achievement and/or well-being information using an established data protocol. A common challenge should not be imposed on the team by outsiders, such as the principal or district leaders, because doing so may compromise the commitment of team members. When teacher teams don't feel consulted about school improvement initiatives, they may be less invested in these efforts. Instead, when team members determine and agree upon a common challenge, there is an increased likelihood that each person will work toward accomplishing it.

In this module, teams are guided through a process to determine a common challenge that is worthy of your time and will positively impact student outcomes. The common challenge is your team's agreed-upon problem of practice, and it drives the work of your team. The Innovation Configuration (IC) Map displayed in Figure 2.1 describes the ideal process for identifying a common challenge for teams to consider while working through this module.

 ◀ **INTRODUCTION TO MODULE 2**
resources.corwin.com/collectiveefficacy

FIGURE 2.1 INNOVATION CONFIGURATION (IC) MAP FOR IDENTIFYING A COMMON CHALLENGE

1: IDEAL STATE	2: DEVELOPING	3: STARTING OUT
The team identifies a common challenge that meets **all** the following criteria.	The team identifies a common challenge that meets **most** (50–99%) of the success criteria.	The team identifies a common challenge that meets **some** (0–50%) of the success criteria.

The common challenge is

- Determined by data
- Publicly acknowledged
- Observable
- Actionable and compelling
- Agreed upon by each team member

At the beginning of each Collective Efficacy Cycle, you are encouraged to reflect on your personal learning. It's important to recognize that teachers' learning is a lifelong process—learning shouldn't stop once we earn a degree or credential. Just as doctors practice medicine and continue to learn from advances in medicine, we should continue to learn from advances in educational research.

◄ TEAMS VISUALIZE THE DESTINATION BY FOLLOWING THE INNOVATION CONFIGURATION MAP
resources.corwin.com/collectiveefficacy

NOTES

_____
_____
_____
_____
_____
_____
_____
_____
_____
_____
_____
_____

ACT 1: WORK HARDER, NOT SMARTER

Tom, the principal at Alta Vista Elementary School, believes that teachers should collaborate regularly to improve student achievement. He has devised a schedule to provide grade-level teacher teams with 60 minutes of common collaboration time every week, which he perceives as a luxury because when he was a teacher, there wasn't any time during the workday to collaborate with colleagues—he had to do everything on his own. Now, as a principal, Tom has hired additional teachers to provide art, music, and PE enrichment to students, so grade-level teams have protected time for planning and collaboration. Tom believes this arrangement will allow teachers the time they need to make data-based decisions that will improve student achievement.

Since the schoolwide focus is on writing, Tom expects each of the grade-level teams to discuss their students' writing and determine ways to make improvements. Tom has emphasized to the fourth-grade teachers that their students' writing is especially critical because of the state-mandated fourth-grade writing test given each year. Tom is very concerned because only 35% of fourth-grade students were proficient on last year's writing test, which was a decrease from 43% proficiency the year before. The superintendent was not pleased with the drop and indicated to Tom that the scores had better increase this year.

According to the schedule, every Thursday after recess, the fourth-grade teachers meet in an empty classroom that is used for professional development. "What are we supposed to do today? Were we supposed to bring something?" Ashley, one of the teachers, asks. Dan replies, "Tom wants us to work on writing, but with being out sick two days and the assembly, I haven't had time for writing." Tamra, the third teacher, stays quiet. She's worked on having students include textual evidence to strengthen their writing, but from experience, she knows that if she speaks up, Ashley and Dan will probably accuse her of being a goody-two-shoes. For the next 60 minutes, Ashley, Dan, and Tamra sit at the same table, but each plans independently of one another.

When teacher teams don't feel consulted about school improvement initiatives, they may be less invested in these efforts.

NOTES

_____

_____

_____

_____

_____

_____

_____

_____

_____

While your team goes through the Collective Efficacy Cycle together each quarter, you are also encouraged to engage in learning on your own and in addition to the evidence-based practice. Jot some notes for yourself in Figure 2.2 about your own learning interests. Are there particular areas you want to learn more about? Perhaps you've heard about Restorative Practices but want to know more. Maybe you want to improve your skill when checking for understanding.

FIGURE 2.2 A MINDFUL MOMENT

What have I noticed about students' academic progress and well-being? What learning interests do I have? What learning will I engage in on my own? What learning can I do with colleagues? What is my or our first step?

WHY TEAMS NEED GOALS

In education and in life, good things begin with a goal: a common challenge unites the team. The common challenge serves as an anchor for the team, helping to ground the work while creating the conditions for team members to uncover potential. These are the enabling conditions for collective efficacy to develop. Without a common challenge, team learning is less efficient.

We want and need to know how we can contribute to advancing student learning. When thinking about using a new strategy to advance student learning, we often ask ourselves these questions:

- What's the purpose?
- What do I need to accomplish?
- How will I do it?
- How am I doing?

Knowing these questions are on our minds, our teams must discuss how each of these questions can be answered by individuals as well as by the collective team. Through these discussions, our team determines what progress and monitoring look like. If student work will be collected as evidence, how and when will that be done? The common challenge is the glue that holds our team together: it provides the purpose and direction. A clear common challenge allows us to monitor our implementation of a strategy, adjust as necessary, and compare the implementation maneuvers we've made with colleagues. Essentially, our learning helps our team turn reflection into public dialogue. Without the glue of a common challenge, our team's commitment to the strategy is likely to wane.

Teachers' learning is a lifelong process—learning shouldn't stop once we earn a degree or credential.

DATA COLLECTION

The first step of the Collective Efficacy Cycle is guided by assessment of student learning and/or well-being. The common challenge is determined after analyzing our students' current performance levels using evidence of learning. It's important that teams don't generalize the needs of the whole class based on the observed needs of a few students. Instead, teams should collaboratively decide what evidence of learning will be collected and analyzed. Sources of this evidence include formal assessments, benchmark assessments, student interviews, tests, quizzes and/or activities, and student voice or observation data.

Teams are encouraged to gather multiple pieces of evidence, even if some of the data overlap because this provides a more complete picture of a student or student group. Evidence can be gathered from four sources:

- Conversations with students
- Observational information
- Student work products
- Formative and/or summative assessments

Use Figure 2.3 to record your thoughts about your team's current data collection and analysis practices. Be specific, as detailed information helps teams to make better decisions.

FIGURE 2.3	INDEPENDENT REFLECTION ABOUT CURRENT DATA COLLECTION AND ANALYSIS PRACTICES	
QUESTION	MY THOUGHTS ABOUT OUR CURRENT PRACTICES	CONSIDERATIONS TO STRENGTHEN OUR PRACTICES
What assessments does our team have access to? What do we use?		
What assessments, or common assessment items, do we discuss as a team?		
What do I want to learn from my colleagues?		
How does our team determine what students already know?		
In what ways do we gather information about student strengths, interests, and talents? How might this information be useful?		
What role does student perception/voice play when we analyze data?		

Use the information from your reflection in Figure 2.3 to begin a conversation with your team about practices of gathering and analyzing data. Take notes in the "My Thoughts" column of Figure 2.4, and then fill in the next column as you discuss your team's thoughts collectively. You can refer to this when deciding your next steps as a team.

◄ A SIXTH-GRADE
TEAM DETERMINES
THE COMMON CHALLENGE
resources.corwin.com/collectiveefficacy

FIGURE 2.4   FOCUSING OUR DATA COLLECTION

QUESTION	MY THOUGHTS	OUR COLLECTIVE THOUGHTS
What is our purpose for gathering these data?		
What data sources will help us to answer our question about current levels of student performance? • Conversations with students • Observational information • Student work products		
When will the pre- and post-data be collected?		

TEAM DATA GATHERING

Once the team has agreed upon the purpose and data to be collected, determine the schedule, and note the people responsible in Figure 2.5. This will ensure that the data is provided and easily accessed at the next meeting.

FIGURE 2.5   DATA COLLECTION SCHEDULE

DATA NEEDED	PERSON(S) RESPONSIBLE	DATE NEEDED

DATA ANALYSIS PROTOCOL

Once a team has gathered enough data, the next step requires an analysis of the data to determine potential steps to move forward. A protocol is often a powerful resource for keeping your team focused and efficient during data analysis.

It is easy and, at times, tempting to veer into topics that are not going to impact student achievement or well-being. A protocol helps teams to avoid deviating from the meeting purpose, which is to uncover what students know and don't know. The following Protocol for Examining Data is adapted from the National School Reform Faculty and may be useful as your team determines a common challenge that is based upon identified student needs.

◄ THE TEAM SELECTS AN EVIDENCE-BASED PRACTICE TO ADDRESS THE COMMON CHALLENGE
resources.corwin.com/collectiveefficacy

Protocol for Examining Data

Suggested Time: 45 minutes

Purpose: This protocol is for use and guiding a group through the analysis of data to identify strengths and common challenges.

Materials: Copies of data for team members, highlighters, chart paper, and the note-taking guides in Figures 2.6 and 2.7

Checklist of Support Activation

- Multiple forms of data are used

- Evidence and research inform decisions

Sample Questions to Support Activation

- How have we used multiple forms of data today to drive our decisions?

- What evidence-based research impacted our decision making?

- What might be other factors that could be impacting the data?

- How do these data affirm what we currently think?

- How do these data disrupt what we currently think and why?

Sample Sentence Starters to Support Activation

- These data are different than what I originally thought because . . .

- A possible cause why the data indicates _____ is _____.

Getting Started: Overview of Data (3 minutes)

Step 1: What parts of these data catch your attention? Just the facts (10 minutes).

Spend 2 minutes silently writing individual observations, 8 minutes discussing as a group.

Step 2: What do the data tell us? What do the data *not* tell us? (10 minutes)

Spend 3 minutes silently making notes, 7 minutes discussing as a group. Make inferences about the data. The activator encourages team members to support their statements with evidence from the data.

Step 3: What good news is there to celebrate? (5 minutes to identify strengths)

The activator asks the group to look for indications of success in the data.

Step 4: What are possible common challenges suggested by the data? (10 minutes)

Use 3 minutes to silently write individual ideas for practice, 7 minutes to discuss as a group. The activator helps the group narrow the list of possible common challenges to no more than 3.

Step 5: What are our key conclusions? (5 minutes)

Identify who will present each of the common challenges in the next protocol.

This sets up the next protocol, which is agreeing on a common challenge for the team.

Source: Adapted from National School Reform Faculty (n.d.).

NOTES

_____

_____

_____

_____

_____

_____

_____

_____

_____

_____

_____

_____

_____

FIGURE 2.6 MY NOTES FROM DATA ANALYSIS PROTOCOL		
QUESTION	MY THOUGHTS	OUR COLLECTIVE THOUGHTS
Step 1: What parts of these data catch our attention? Just the facts.		
Step 2: What do the data tell us? What do the data *not* tell us?		
Step 3: What good news is there to celebrate?		
Step 4: What are possible common challenges suggested by the data?		
Step 5: What are our key conclusions?		

FIGURE 2.7 MY NOTES TO NARROW DOWN POSSIBLE COMMON CHALLENGES

POSSIBLE COMMON CHALLENGES	WHO WILL PRESENT THIS CHALLENGE TO THE GROUP?

COMMON CHALLENGE PROTOCOL

Now that there is an understanding of current student proficiency levels, areas of strength, and places for improvement, your team can identify a common challenge. Use the quality checklist shown in Figure 2.8 to monitor the development of the common challenge to be investigated.

FIGURE 2.8 COMMON CHALLENGE QUALITY CHECKLIST

☐ Is the common challenge grounded in the data?

☐ Is the common challenge observable and actionable?

☐ Will addressing the common challenge make a significant difference in students' learning and/or well-being?

☐ Is the common challenge something that the team is curious about?

☐ Does the common challenge mobilize and motivate the team to engage in the work?

NOTES

_____

_____

_____

_____

_____

_____

_____

_____

Once your PLC team has developed a quality common challenge, effective and efficient progress toward addressing that common challenge requires you to fine-tune your work together. This tuning process helps avoid common challenges that are too big or too broad, that have too much packed into a single challenge, or that are related to something outside the limits of the team.

Common Challenge Tuning Protocol

Suggested Time: Up to 25 minutes per possible common challenge

Purpose: There are times when the PLC+ team as a whole will share a common challenge and other times when an individual team member is looking for the support of their colleagues. The following protocol can be used to explore the common challenge at both levels.

Materials: The activator will need to gather or delegate the gathering of all materials, such as chart paper, highlighters, sticky notes, and other resources, to engage in this process.

Getting Started: Identify an activator for this protocol, and assign a timekeeper and, if desired, a recorder. Because the activator is assisting the team and moving the discussion forward, we advise that the activator not simultaneously serve as a presenter. Another activator can assume this role during this time.

Step 1: Presenter shares common challenge and describes (5 minutes)

- Where it came from; who was involved in identifying it and its connection to data

- Context of other school or district efforts to address a problem

Step 2: Team members ask factual clarifying questions (5 minutes).

Step 3: Presenter steps back (remains silent 8 to 10 minutes) while team members provide

- **Warm feedback:** Aspects of the common challenge that, based on the criteria and list of potential challenges, make them think this will work well to address student needs

- **Cool feedback:** Concerns or suggestions about the common challenge, including suggestions for fine-tuning

- **Stretches:** Other things the presenter may not have thought about but might support the goals of the PLC+

Step 4: Presenter rejoins for general discussion (balance of 25 minutes' time), including

- Responses and factual clarifications by presenter
- Feedback from team members focused on supporting the common challenge and not to be taken personally; it is not an evaluation of an individual teacher but rather a collective brainstorm to respond to the common challenge
- Reflections by all participants about what they learned

Step 5: Repeat the common challenge protocol to discuss the next proposed challenge.

NOTES

_____

_____

_____

_____

_____

_____

_____

_____

_____

_____

_____

_____

_____

_____

_____

_____

_____

_____

_____

_____

_____

_____

REACHING CONSENSUS ON THE COMMON CHALLENGE

Once all the possible common challenges have been discussed, it is time to reach an agreement on the one that will drive your team's inquiry cycle.

Step 1: Consider the possible common challenges.

- What are the relative strengths of and barriers to each?
- How does each possible challenge rate on the common challenge quality checklist in Figure 2.8?

Step 2: Propose a common challenge.

- Members formulate a proposed common challenge, amending it to reflect the discussion.
- Members work together to solve problems and to fine-tune the proposed common challenge.
- Test for agreement:
  - I will fully support our inquiry cycle investigating this common challenge.
  - I am in support of my colleagues' decision.
  - I will not block this decision.

The activator asks, "Are there any further questions or concerns about the common challenge we have selected?" If there is no further discussion, then agreement has been reached. If there is a call of concern, the person raising the concern re-examines by repeating Steps 1 and 2.

Step 3: Debrief the process using a plus/delta system. Make notes about refinements for future processes in Figure 2.9.

- What did the group do well?
- What could have been improved?

NOTES

_____

_____

_____

_____

_____

_____

_____

FIGURE 2.9 DEBRIEFING THE PROCESS

Our common challenge for this inquiry cycle is:

Date:

Notes for future refinements:

Step 4: Plan for collecting evidence.

Now that your team has identified your common challenge, you might develop or adopt a common assessment that will be used as an initial assessment and as a post-assessment (see Figure 2.10). Or you can agree to collect another type of evidence, such as writing samples, self-assessment data, or vocabulary charts. Teams involved in a Collective Efficacy Cycle may include teachers who teach different subjects or grade levels. The key is that they have a common challenge and can collect evidence about the impact of their efforts. A cross-department team may collect student writing that reflects the instruction students received on writing claim, evidence, and reasoning papers across English, science, history, and technical subjects. A cross-grade-level team may want to focus on vocabulary development across a three-year span (for example, third-, fourth-, and fifth-grade teachers) to see how their efforts are impacting learning. Sometimes teams create their own assessments, and other times there are tools available that can be used for this purpose. Collecting evidence allows your team to gauge the impact of your efforts and to monitor the progress and achievement of students.

FIGURE 2.10   INITIAL AND POST-ASSESSMENT PLANS

Initial and Post-Assessment:

Date, Time, Location(s):

Materials Needed:

Source: Adapted from City et al. (2010).

A NOTE ABOUT SCHOOL-BASED DATA DISCUSSIONS

The Collective Efficacy Cycle is powerful because it is determined by a teacher team. This marks a shift from the thinking that school-based data teams must be formally commissioned to analyze data and publish long-range plans for the school community. While well-intended to make data-based decisions to improve student learning, these plans usually fall flat, and often quickly. According to Heather Hill, a researcher at the Harvard Graduate School of Education, an examination of 10 recent research studies on whole-team data discussions indicates that there were "zero impacts of getting teachers to be really productive, understand what kids don't know, and change their instruction" (as cited by Geller, 2021).

The problem with data-centric discussions is that there is a tendency for well-intentioned teachers to rationalize and justify students' low performance. After looking at a summative assessment, a teacher may make comments such as "Juan was having a bad week during testing. That's why he didn't do well on the assessment" and "That test is poorly written. It's no wonder the kids can't show what they know." While these statements may be true, teachers are less apt to do anything different in their classrooms after sitting through whole-team data discussions in which the data are explained away. In fact, data teams spend about 85% of their time focused on why the students did or did not perform well and only 15% of their time on actions that they can take to improve learning (Evans et al., 2019). Further, group conversations often drift toward strategies with limited impact, such as using a worksheet or trying a different activity with students. Since teachers and administrators often feel that there isn't enough time, they resort to quick fixes (Geller, 2021).

◄ HOW TEAMS CAN AVOID BEING OVERWHELMED BY DATA
resources.corwin.com/collectiveefficacy

In addition to teachers not gaining high-impact instructional wisdom from these data-focused meetings, valuable time is consumed. Sitting through unproductive meetings results in many lost opportunities to be responsive to students' needs. Instead of engaging in perfunctory data-centric conversations, teachers' time could be better spent engaging in more relevant conversations that encourage them to reflect on their teaching practices. For example, it might be useful for teachers to discuss what high-quality teaching really means by engaging in a microteaching session in which a teacher shares a video clip and talks through the thinking that is represented in each instructional move. Of course, these discussions should include evidence of student learning using work samples and other relevant pieces of data.

While data-centric meetings may not be the best use of teachers' precious time, it's not to say that we shouldn't look at the data. A more meaningful approach is to provide time for teachers to analyze student achievement and guide their self-reflections, focusing the conversation on what needs to be done to ensure learning.

TEAM-DRIVEN SCHOOL STRENGTHENING

A focus on a shared goal by a group of educators is what sets the Collective Efficacy Cycle model apart from other collaborative professional learning experiences. Shared goals are driving forces for how team members will allocate their resources and time to achieve the goal. Goals are essential and serve as a public acknowledgment of the team's commitment to the improvement area. However, it doesn't work as well when goals are imposed upon teams by external agencies or authorities. When this occurs, there is less commitment to the goal because teachers don't feel a sense of ownership. Rather, when team members develop and agree upon a shared goal, there is a stronger likelihood that everyone will take steps to achieve the goal.

NOTES

_____

_____

_____

_____

_____

_____

_____

_____

_____

_____

_____

_____

_____

_____

_____

_____

_____

_____

_____

_____

_____

_____

_____

ACT 2: WORK SMARTER, NOT HARDER

Tom, the principal at Alta Vista Elementary School, believes that teachers should collaborate regularly to improve student achievement. To that end, he and the school's Instructional Leadership Team researched the value of teacher collaboration and jointly determined how they could structure instructional time to support teams to work together to improve student learning. As a result of these conversations, additional teachers were hired to provide art, music, and PE enrichment to students so grade-level teams could have protected time for planning and collaboration. Tom and the Instructional Leadership Team then devised a schedule that provides grade-level teacher teams with 60 minutes of common collaboration time every week.

Every Thursday after recess, the fourth-grade teachers meet in an empty classroom that is used for professional learning. When they arrive, the space is set up with a projector and other materials for teams to quickly access, such as chart paper, markers, sticky notes, and the district's established pacing guides. The team already knows what's on today's agenda because Ashley provided a draft and asked for input from Dan and Tamra on Monday. She then finalized the agenda and uploaded it to a shared folder where the team could access it.

Today, Ashley, Dan, and Tamra have brought students' informative writing about extreme weather, as this was the topic decided by the team at last week's collaboration session. They are reading students' work from each other's classes and are making piles according to the established success criteria when Tom walks into the room. "Hey everyone, how did writing go this week? When I visited your classrooms, I noticed that kids were using at least one source to write about extreme weather. That was so cool! And, when I was in Tamra's class, I saw that students were partnered up to peer edit. Each student had their own checklist of the success criteria. I was blown away by how the kids could guide each other to add more details or to improve the organization. What are you finding as you read the papers?"

MODULE 2 RECAP: WHAT DID WE LEARN?

Yay, team! Now that you've used data to determine a common challenge, your team is beginning to cultivate collective efficacy in a systematic way.

Consider any specific team actions that felt efficacious and note them in Figure 2.11. Questions to consider in this reflection that are related to the common challenge include:

◀ COLLECTIVE EFFICACY REFLECTION
resources.corwin.com/collectiveefficacy

- Did we collect initial assessment data?

- Did we identify students' strengths and needs?

FIGURE 2.11 COLLECTIVE EFFICACY CYCLE REFLECTIVE QUESTIONS

QUESTION	MY THOUGHTS/DEGREE OF COLLECTIVE EFFICACY				
Mastery Experiences: In what ways was our team successful? Identify specific instances when our actions were skillful.	1	2	3	4	5
Trust: Was there a sense of trust among the team while determining the common challenge? Note instances when trust was strong.	1	2	3	4	5
Problem Solving: In what ways did we work together to solve problems? Describe when and how the team supported each other.	1	2	3	4	5
Assets-Orientation: When faced with a problem, did we maintain an assets-oriented stance? Note any situations when the team built upon students' strengths, interests, and background knowledge.	1	2	3	4	5
Efficiency: Did we adhere to agreed-upon protocols and use our time well? Write down times when our meetings felt productive.	1	2	3	4	5
Optimism: What was the general tenor/emotional tone of our meetings? Describe instances when we supported each other to maintain a positive outlook.	1	2	3	4	5

online resources

Access videos and resources for this module at
resources.corwin.com/collectiveefficacy

Module 3
BUILDING EDUCATOR KNOWLEDGE AND SKILLS

MODULE OVERVIEW

Now that the team has identified a common challenge, we turn our attention to the implications for *our* learning. During this module, team members are invited to reflect on themselves as learners and engage in team-directed experiences that build knowledge and elevate professional skills.

It's important to recognize that educators' learning is a lifelong process. We don't simply repeat the same things year after year. Ten years of teaching experience does not mean one year repeated 10 times. We learn, grow, and change as our experiences with students and colleagues widen. The Innovation Configuration (IC) Map displayed in Figure 3.1 provides a description of what the ideal process for learning an evidence-based practice looks like as teams work through a Collective Efficacy Cycle.

◀ INTRODUCTION TO MODULE 3
resources.corwin.com/collectiveefficacy

FIGURE 3.1   INNOVATION CONFIGURATION (IC) MAP FOR BUILDING EDUCATOR KNOWLEDGE AND SKILLS

1: IDEAL STATE	2: DEVELOPING	3: STARTING OUT
The team learns a professional skill or strategy by meeting **all** of the following criteria.	The team learns a professional skill or strategy by meeting **most** (50–99%) of the success criteria.	The team learns a professional skill or strategy by meeting **some** (0–49%) of the success criteria.

A teaching skill/strategy is furthered through

- Investigation of evidence-based practices published by a reputable source

- Selection of an evidence-based practice that addresses the common challenge

- Professional reading(s)

- Team discussion

- Modeling and/or think-alouds that support the implementation of the practice

There are times when we sense a disconnect between what teachers want and what administrators want. It's possible that both groups want the same thing, but cultural norms and ineffective communication prevent both groups from seeing eye to eye. In the following vignette, you'll learn of a middle school where teachers and administrators are on two different pages about professional development (PD). The teachers want to use PD time to work on progress reports and the administrators want teachers to learn about a growth mindset. While reading, we invite you to consider how this situation might be handled such that there's shared agreement as to how PD time could be best utilized to meet everyone's needs. Later in the module, we provide an updated vignette that describes how PD at this middle school might look with a little bit of reorganization.

NOTES

_____
_____
_____
_____
_____
_____
_____

ACT 1: WORK HARDER, NOT SMARTER

It's 1:30 on a Wednesday afternoon in October, a week before progress reports are due. The seventh-grade English teachers, Lily, Lourdes, and Barb, are headed to their school's multi-purpose room for PD. There is mandatory training for two hours each quarter and according to the message that was emailed to them on Monday afternoon, today's training is about having a "growth mindset." As they walk, Lily says, "Um . . . I don't really know why we have to do this right now. Progress reports go home next week. Don't they know how long it takes to read 170 students' papers?" The others nod in agreement, also wishing they could use the next two hours to score students' essays and get a start on the progress reports. They settle into their seats for another "sit-and-get" PD.

In contrast to the seventh-grade English teachers, the school's administrators are excited about today's PD. They went to a conference that promoted having a growth mindset and it was *so amazing* that an external consultant was contracted to bring the PD to the school. The administrators are sure teachers will be delighted with this training and will want to apply it in their classrooms right away. They are almost giddy as they introduce the speaker, but their enthusiasm begins to wane when they notice the teachers aren't interested in what the speaker says about a growth mindset. The teachers aren't rude, but their body language indicates that they are disengaged.

Two hours later, the PD concludes. None of the teachers asks questions of the speaker nor lingers in the multi-purpose room. Lily, Lourdes, and Barb walk out to their cars together, discussing the PD and agreeing that it was another waste of time. Other small groups of teachers are clustered throughout the parking lot, each involved in their own conversations. For teachers at this middle school, the parking lot is where they critique the PD.

Meanwhile, back in the school office, the administrators are disheartened by the teachers' lack of enthusiasm throughout the PD. They feel that this is yet another example of how the teachers are indifferent to students' needs. The administrators conclude that the teachers are stuck in their ways and that the PD session was a big waste of money.

> **When growth isn't valued or recognized, we risk teachers viewing teaching as a dead-end job.**

YEARS OF TEACHING WITH AUTONOMY

Typically, novice teachers are expected to become strong teachers on their own. There is often little coaching or other support provided as teachers find their footing during those first years in the profession. Those who persist and become experienced teachers are rewarded with additional alone time. This isolation, which is frequently coveted as a teacher's right, also restricts growth, support, and recognition. While isolation may foster individual creativity, it also robs teachers of opportunities to collaborate with peers and perhaps of valuable support to improve throughout their careers. Significantly, isolation "denies teachers recognition that can only come from someone who is present at the work and prepared to assess it" (Bird & Little, 1986, p. 495).

Teaching is difficult to do and watch at the same time; a teacher may spend more than thirty-five years without really ever *seeing* their best work. And since teachers are rarely afforded opportunities to watch each other teach, their own experience may blind them to new or different strategies to try. Without a shared understanding of a particular strategy, two teachers may believe that they are implementing the strategy in the same way, but, in fact, are not. Without observation and dialogue, this misunderstanding often goes unchecked. This lack of shared understanding of what one another is doing limits professional growth.

FIGURE 3.2 A MINDFUL MOMENT

Are you familiar with the instructional practices and emotional environment in your colleagues' classrooms? What do you know from firsthand experience? Or is your knowledge based on what they tell you? What would you like to know?

As teachers gain experience and become more skilled, it's important that their growth is acknowledged by others, including peers and administrators. When growth isn't valued or recognized, we risk teachers viewing teaching as a dead-end job. They may still care about students, but teachers might also feel that PD and other school improvement efforts are a waste of their time. This phenomenon is further intensified if there is burnout or low morale in the school. Teachers who are running on empty or are pushed to the brink of exhaustion need substantive support systems. Given the complexity of teaching and the norm of autonomy, many teachers are likely not getting the support needed to be the teachers they could be. They may feel isolated and alone. It's clear that the disadvantages of working in isolation far outweigh the benefits.

Teachers who work together often gain an increased sense of mastery with each year of teaching.

Teachers who work together can boost each other's careers. It is often stimulating to work with other adults, those who share a common purpose and face many of the same challenges. Additionally, teachers who work together often gain an increased sense of mastery with each year of teaching. There's increased recognition of the benefits of teaming. It's evident that successful teaching is a shared accomplishment (Sparks, 2013).

The most significant resource for school improvement is in our classrooms: teachers. Time that is devoted for teachers to study, collaborate, and analyze teaching and learning advances professional practices and student learning. Further, when working together, teachers often gain a needed system of professional support at the school site.

Schools that establish regular opportunities for teachers to discuss student learning and reflect upon their teaching strategies often foster cultures that are supportive in ways that extend beyond congeniality. In these situations, team members support and mentor each other and collaboratively determine solutions when students struggle to learn. A team that works together, sharing the responsibility of educating students, has a higher likelihood of not letting learners slip through the cracks.

EVIDENCE-BASED PRACTICES

While teachers use a variety of instructional methods with students, some are more effective than others. The strength of strategies is gauged by published academic research that has been conducted with students. While research has been available to educators for decades, accessing studies and making sense of them may have been a challenge. In recent years, however, this information has been disseminated freely and publicly in the form of electronic databases that allow users to easily search, sort, and filter through the evidence.

It's important to note that although the terms *research* and *evidence-based practices* are sometimes used interchangeably, there are differences between the two; each has a different purpose.

◄ NANCY PROVIDES INSIGHTS ABOUT EVIDENCE-BASED PRACTICES
resources.corwin.com/collectiveefficacy

Research is used to conduct an investigation, the results of which are added to existing evidence. Conversely, evidence-based practices are determined by the appraisal of the strongest evidence. This means that with a few clicks, we can have evidence at our fingertips. Educators can now locate evidence-based practices that have a strong likelihood of accelerating student learning.

We'll recommend two respected sources educators can access for evidence-based practices: Visible Learning Meta[X] and the What Works Clearinghouse. Each meets rigorous standards and provides different resources, as noted in Figure 3.3.

FIGURE 3.3   DATABASES TO FIND EVIDENCE-BASED PRACTICES

VISIBLE LEARNING META[X]	WHAT WORKS CLEARINGHOUSE
• Videos	• Practice guides
• Webinars	• Webinars
• Gold papers	• Tutorials
• White papers	• Infographics
• Infographics	• Videos
• Tools	• Tools

While the Visible Learning evidence base and the What Works Clearinghouse provide evidence-based practices, other resources can assist your team with learning and planning. It's important that a process is put into place so teams can appraise materials for their quality. Much like a learning log, Figure 3.4 offers teams a place to record their learning and next steps.

NOTES

_____

_____

_____

_____

_____

_____

_____

_____

_____

_____

FIGURE 3.4 LEARNING LOG			
QUESTION(S) BEING EXPLORED	RESOURCE	WHAT IS LEARNED?	FURTHER QUESTIONS/ NEXT STEPS

SCHEDULED TIME FOR PROFESSIONAL LEARNING

Schools schedule time for educators' learning in many ways. For example, some arrange daily schedules to allow for common planning times when teachers can meet during the workday. Districts may hire substitute teachers to allow teachers to meet in learning teams or to observe peers. Others fund stipends for teacher learning outside the regular workday. Districts may "bank" time, allowing educators shorter workdays and combining the extra minutes for a block of professional development. While it's understood that teachers have professional learning needs, teachers are often required to attend professional development activities that feel disconnected from their day-to-day needs in the classroom. Instead, effective professional learning that results in both enhanced teacher practices and student achievement can be planned and implemented by adhering to key design elements.

THE SEVEN DESIGN ELEMENTS OF EFFECTIVE PROFESSIONAL LEARNING

Effective professional learning that elevates teaching practices and student outcomes entails more than dark chocolate and Diet Coke. As with students, treats and other material rewards only get you so far. The Learning Policy Institute (Darling-Hammond, 2017) defines effective professional development as "structured professional learning that results in changes to teacher knowledge and practices, and improvements in student learning outcomes" (p. 2). Further, this organization has conducted a rigorous investigation of published educational research over many decades to determine and illuminate the specific features of effective professional learning. From this analysis, the authors contend that effective professional learning shares seven design elements.

◄ THE SEVEN DESIGN ELEMENTS
OF PROFESSIONAL LEARNING
resources.corwin.com/collectiveefficacy

These seven elements require that professional learning

1. Is discipline-specific
2. Engages people through active learning strategies
3. Provides models of effective practice
4. Supports collaboration
5. Provides coaching and expert support
6. Offers feedback and reflection
7. Is of sustained duration

Successful professional learning models typically employ these seven elements simultaneously. When effectively implemented, well-designed professional learning experiences can foster desirable changes in teacher practice and student outcomes. A PLC+ team is an example of a professional learning model that incorporates many, if not all, of the design elements identified by the Learning Policy Institute. Further, a Collective Efficacy Cycle is a way for teams to harness their expertise by designing and implementing their own professional learning. When designing professional learning, teams ought to consider the design elements recommended by the Learning Policy Institute in Figure 3.5, as well as the pitfalls to avoid from traditional PD practices.

FIGURE 3.5	SEVEN DESIGN ELEMENTS OF EFFECTIVE PROFESSIONAL LEARNING AND PITFALLS TO AVOID	
DESIGN ELEMENT	DESCRIPTION AND KEY IDEAS	PITFALLS TO AVOID
1. Is discipline-specific	Learning is focused on the content that teachers teach. • There is job-embedded learning. • Experiences are situated within the context of teachers' classrooms and current students.	PD is generic. • PD is delivered by outsiders. • PD is divorced from teachers' classroom or school context.
2. Engages people through active learning strategies	Professional learning addresses *how* teachers learn as well as *what* teachers learn. • Teachers' experience is utilized as a resource for new learning. • Adults choose learning opportunities based on their interests and needs. • Authentic artifacts, such as student work products, help teachers to construct learning that refines their practice.	PD is "done" through sit-and-get sessions. • Learning is passive. • Teachers' previous experience is disregarded. • New strategies are layered on top of the old.
3. Provides models of effective practice	A vision of practice is provided to teachers. • Curricular models are provided. • Instructional models are provided. • Expert support and coaching are available.	Teachers refer to curriculum guides for support. • Teachers who utilize curriculum materials alone have lower student achievement than teachers who access materials *and* expert support.

(Continued)

FIGURE 3.5 (CONTINUED)

4. Supports collaboration	Collective work in trusting environments provides a foundation for inquiry and reflection. • Grade levels, departments, and schools are the basis of teams who problem solve and learn together. • The equity of whole systems improves.	Individualistic work can be isolating. • There is a business-as-usual approach. • PD is a single or isolated encounter.
5. Provides coaching and expert support	Experts, typically educators themselves, play a critical role by guiding and supporting colleagues. • Strategies are modeled. • Support for group processing and discussion is available. • Collaborative analysis of student learning is promoted. • Coaching (can occur in a teacher's classroom) is offered.	Teachers are on their own to implement new curricula, tools, and approaches.
6. Offers feedback and reflection	There is built-in time for teachers to think about and adjust their practice. • There is intentional time for feedback and reflection.	Feedback to teachers may be limited or misaligned with teachers' learning needs. • Reflection may or may not occur.
7. Is of sustained duration	Meaningful professional learning that leads to changes in practice takes time. • Professional learning is rigorous, cumulative, and organized around a single set of concepts or practices. • Learning may last for weeks, months, or longer as teachers apply and refine their practice.	PD does not afford the time necessary for teachers to learn at deep levels.

If we truly want to improve teaching and learning, it's imperative that educators are given voice to provide input about school improvement efforts. Professional learning is most effective when it is identified collaboratively by teachers as they reflect on their practices and student learning needs. When educators engage in professional learning experiences with their colleagues, they can learn from each other, support one another, and hold each other accountable for applying what they learn. Learning throughout the school year makes it easier for educators to apply what they learn right away so students can benefit immediately.

When teachers take an active role in choosing and designing learning experiences that facilitate their own and their team's learning, they are building upon their beliefs, backgrounds, experiences, motivation, interests, and professional identities—all of which increase the quality of professional learning. Decisions that are made internally can pinpoint exactly what is needed, taking into consideration all phases of the learning process. Learning Forward (2017) reminds us that teacher teams who design professional learning experiences consider the best ways for the team members to deepen knowledge, increase skills, transform practice, question attitudes and beliefs, and inspire action that leads to improved student outcomes.

When learning a new cognitive skill, it's also important that teams are mindful of the relationship between emotions and cognition, because emotions impact learning whether we're aware of them or not. Immordino-Yang (2016) asserts that we should pay attention to the adults' learning climate for five reasons:

1. Emotions facilitate cognitive learning

2. Emotional connections to learning can be conscious or unconscious

3. Emotional learning shapes future behavior

4. The most effective and efficient learning incorporates emotion into the cognitive knowledge being built

5. Without emotion, learning is impaired (pp. 96–99)

Since learning is mediated by emotions, it's important to intentionally cultivate positive emotions so optimal adult learning can occur. Use Figure 3.6 to reflect on the team's current emotional state. Often, it's helpful to consider the ways in which people want to be acknowledged. Some people appreciate an empathetic listener they can trust to share and process their fears—this is heart work. Others prefer intellectual stimulation—they wish to use their heads to solve problems. Still others want to take action—they wish to do something with their hands. This could be creating an anchor chart for others or sketching out a lesson sequence. Based upon your knowledge of your team members' preferences, determine possible ways you might engage, and re-engage, people by appealing to their heads, hearts, and hands when learning something new.

FIGURE 3.6 APPEALING TO THE HEAD, HEART, AND HANDS WHEN LEARNING SOMETHING NEW

	CURRENT EMOTIONAL STATE	POSSIBLE WAYS TO IMPROVE USING HEAD, HEART, AND/OR HANDS
My Needs		
My Team Members' Needs		

New learning and follow-ups are more effective when people's personal and emotional needs are tended to. Demonstrations, discussions, and lesson development are all ways learning can move forward while nurturing the team's learning climate.

Demonstrations and discussions are opportunities that keep new learning at the forefront, skillfully weaving the strategy, knowledge, or behavior into the flow of a teacher's normal practice. To this end, teachers are offered the freedom to make the new learning their own and to find the value of it within their own classroom contexts, in ways that align with their personal teaching styles and preferences. When we design for this type of learning, we are factoring in duration and frequency of practice, which are crucial for new learning to assimilate and become a natural part of the teacher's repertoire (Joyce, 2016).

Additionally, there is a need for teachers and administrators to work together to shape the school's culture, policies, and practices in ways that support both adult and student learning (see also Figure 3.7). When this type of collaboration occurs, teachers lead from their classrooms, monitoring and supporting the instructional practices of their peers. Teachers often have pedagogical and content knowledge that their principals may lack. Indeed, in every school, there is a "sleeping giant of teacher leadership, which can be a strong catalyst for making change" (Katzenmeyer & Moller, 2009, p. 6).

Teachers often have pedagogical and content knowledge that their principals may lack.

NOTES

_____

_____

_____

_____

_____

_____

_____

_____

_____

_____

_____

_____

_____

_____

_____

FIGURE 3.7   A MINDFUL MOMENT

Have you been asked to be a part of a school improvement strategy session? If so, what were the circumstances? What was the result? What are one or two takeaways that can be applied to a new learning situation?

PURPOSEFUL COLLABORATION

In high-performance learning cultures, teachers are guided by inquiry, become increasingly knowledgeable, and understand the benefits of purposeful collaboration. Collaboration is a powerful way to expand educators' capacity and increase the professional capital in the school while harnessing the power of the collective (Sharratt & Planche, 2016). This type of movement empowers teachers to pursue a clear moral purpose: to enhance student learning. Effective professional learning helps students to thrive. It serves as a catalyst for student learning growth because students taught by the most effective teachers learn in six months what other students may learn in a year. It cultivates a culture of improvement and is bolstered by a shared commitment to high-quality teaching and learning.

Students taught by the most effective teachers learn in six months what other students may learn in a year.

When the school culture values collaborative professionalism, teachers become detectives of their own practice. They analyze details and work together to pinpoint evidence-based solutions to common challenges and other problems of practice. This type of purposeful and supportive collaboration takes teaching practices to new heights that are impossible to reach alone. Reflect upon experiences when you've been successful and note those in Figure 3.8. Consider sharing those with your team.

NOTES

_____
_____
_____
_____
_____
_____
_____
_____
_____
_____
_____
_____
_____
_____
_____

FIGURE 3.8 PERSONAL AND TEAM GROWTH

QUESTION	MY THOUGHTS	MY TEAM'S THOUGHTS
How do you encourage yourself when you're trying something new?		
What new opportunities have come out of challenges you've faced?		
How can you step outside your comfort zone to grow?		
Describe a time when you stayed focused and clear of distractions.		

COLLECTIVE RESPONSIBILITY

Teachers who believe they make a difference in children's lives feel personally responsible for every student in their classes. When teachers share their teaching practices with colleagues and look for opportunities for purposeful collaboration, they contribute to a culture of collective responsibility. Collective responsibility is a crucial shift toward improving instructional practices and lays the foundation for collective efficacy, as well as gains in student achievement.

Additionally, collective responsibility fosters an ethic of reflective practice. Reflection founded on continuous improvement is an effective form of professional learning. It's important that teachers regularly pause and take stock of how things are going, talk with students and colleagues, and determine what's been successful and what changes are needed.

STUDENT LEARNING NEEDS DRIVE ADULT LEARNING NEEDS

Since your team has identified your common challenge, your team members are likely gathering initial common formative assessment data. In addition to this evidence, team members can take this time to observe student learning patterns and talk to students about their learning. Students can use the lesson or unit's success criteria as a reference point to discuss their progress with peers and their teachers. Teachers gain much when listening to students' perceptions of learning. This helps teachers to better know their students and how to best meet their needs.

All schools should be places where both adults and students learn.

All schools should be places where both adults and students learn. Effective teaching doesn't occur by accident but is the result of study, reflection, practice, and hard work. But teachers often resent one-size-fits-all workshops that are irrelevant to their needs and their students' needs. Professional learning that is poorly conceived often leaves a bad taste in teachers' mouths.

The effectiveness of professional learning depends on how carefully educators conceive, plan, and implement it. This requires rigorous thinking and execution. Less experienced educators interact with and learn from more experienced educators on the team, but they can also coach more experienced teachers by mediating their thinking. As all members of the team become more skilled, they reduce or eliminate implementation variations and begin to take collective responsibility for the success of all students, rather than just their own. Use Figure 3.9 to brainstorm your students' and your own learning needs.

FIGURE 3.9 ACTIVATING LEARNING FOR MYSELF AND OTHERS

What are my students' learning needs?	What do I need to learn so that I can best support my students' learning needs?	What learning will I engage in to meet my learning needs?
What have I noticed about students' progress toward standards?	What strategies might I need to learn more about?	What learning can I do on my own? What can I do with colleagues?

IDENTIFY STUDENT MISCONCEPTIONS

Teams can refine their teaching practices by collectively identifying student misconceptions and discussing how learners arrived at them. This can be done prior to engaging in instruction or after evidence has been collected. When it is done prior to instruction, teams can develop a proactive instructional response to address these issues head on. Data from prior units with current students and trend data are useful for teams to discuss. This is a powerful way to provide students with a focused and immediate response.

While we can't identify all the potential misconceptions learners might have, identifying common patterns together strengthens the expertise of the team. Teams can also identify and diagnose student misconceptions after data has been collected. This helps teams to determine current gaps in learning and develop appropriate instructional responses to move student learning forward. Figure 3.10 offers your team a place to brainstorm initial thoughts about how to address student misconceptions.

FIGURE 3.10   IDENTIFYING STUDENT MISCONCEPTIONS

COMMON CHALLENGE:

COMMON STUDENT MISCONCEPTIONS	INSTRUCTIONAL RESPONSE	POSSIBLE STRATEGIES

It's also important that teacher teams keep abreast of current educational research. There are new standards, new curricula, and new ways of learning—it's not a matter of just polishing the old comfortable ways of teaching (Joyce, 2016). This means that learning is ongoing and illustrates the importance of following up through mechanisms for internal accountability. After, or during, a learning experience, teams must determine how to check in with each other about the new knowledge, skill, or strategy. Without established follow-ups, many teachers may return to old habits.

Teachers have the capacity to be agents of school change and their efforts are particularly more effective when collective teacher efficacy is built and nurtured through structures that support and further collaborative professional learning. When there are high levels of collective teacher efficacy on PLC+ teams and in schools, people take ownership of the shared agreements and enforce them. The norms of working in isolation are replaced by the values of teamwork and collaboration.

When there are feelings that "we can do this together," the impetus for continuing the learning and deepening the work emerges internally, not from outsiders or authority figures. In these schools, teachers support each other by listening, discussing, clarifying, and developing collective expertise. Their sense of collective efficacy develops.

INPUT TRAINING

The following sections detail three forms of input training that teams use to learn together and jointly improve teaching practices and student learning outcomes:

- Professional reading
- Modeling and think-alouds
- Role-plays

Source 1: Professional Reading

Professional readings come in the form of books, modules, articles, blogs, and other sources of print information. There is an abundance of free information available on the Internet, though it varies in quality and relevance. While almost everything you find in an online search yields information, it can be overwhelming to locate and zero in on reputable sources related to a particular interest or teaching strategy. The PLC+ team structure helps because it is designed to center on a particular common challenge through inquiry, allowing team members to be more focused in their search for professional readings that can be reviewed by your team.

Based on the common challenge, your team determines one or two professional readings to focus on during the Collective Efficacy Cycle (see Figure 3.11). The reading should be directly linked to content knowledge or a strategy that helps your team solve the common challenge. Often these passages are downloaded and printed so that people can reread and refer to them throughout the Collective Efficacy Cycle. Since the expectation is that your team learns together, you will continue to revisit the reading throughout the Collective Efficacy Cycle as your collective knowledge increases.

Your team determines if the reading will occur prior to or during a meeting, as both ways have benefits. We recommend text-based discussion protocols so that your time is used effectively. A source for text-based discussion protocols is the National School Reform Faculty at nsfharmony.org. During discussions, people can refer to the thoughts they've jotted down and connections they made while reading. Team members also frequently note questions that arise for them in the margins so that they might ask team members later. Because the reading and discussions are focused, people learn collaboratively and often feel a greater sense of confidence and competence.

◄ LEARNING ABOUT AN
EVIDENCE-BASED PRACTICE
resources.corwin.com/collectiveefficacy

FIGURE 3.11 PROFESSIONAL READING SOURCE

Ideas for Professional Readings	
Books, Blogs, and Other Resources We Have Access to	

Text-Based Protocols

A protocol is a defined set of actions used for a specific purpose. Typically, protocols are structured in a step-by-step manner that allows people to dig deeper into a particular concept. The protocol gives shape to an activity by telling participants what they must do, how they must do it, and provides the time frames for each step.

During Collective Efficacy Cycles, it's important that teams stay current by dedicating time to read and discuss articles, blogs, book modules, and other sources of professional literature related to evidence-based instruction. Usually, text-based protocols require people to read a passage or text more than one time. This provides multiple exposures to the meaning of the text, thus allowing people to mull over ideas and comprehend at deeper levels. Often, text-based protocols have a discussion component, making them collaborative by design. Using this type of structure gives shape to a reading activity so that people have professional learning experiences together and opportunities to make sense of new ideas or concepts.

Discussion-Based Protocols

In addition to text-based discussion protocols, there are also discussion-based protocols that provide a structure for people to use during professional reading opportunities. Discussion-based protocols are useful for learners of all ages, though some are better suited for adults than children, and vice versa. When each person understands and agrees to use a particular protocol, people are often able to work more effectively, both independently and collaboratively. Sometimes the structure of a discussion-based protocol will spark new thinking that may not have been otherwise considered.

While there might be an independent thinking aspect to a protocol, most protocols are collaborative in nature. For example, people may be asked to first consider a response independently to a question posed by a facilitator. Then, people are paired up and are given 3 minutes each to explain their responses. Finally, pairs are arranged into quads for a larger discussion. With each round, people deepen their understanding of the topic by listening to and considering others' perspectives. Discussion-based protocols also offer ways to scaffold learning for those with less background knowledge as well and often can be extended for those who have more advanced knowledge. Discussion-based protocols are useful for teams to utilize when making decisions and coming to a consensus. Simply put, protocols provide the rules for discussion so there can be equity of voice.

Professional Knowledge

In addition to reading about ways to address the common challenge, your team will also begin to formulate these understandings into application in their own classrooms. Your team meeting is a safe space for teachers to speculate how an evidence-based strategy will positively affect student learning or role-play the strategy to get a feel for it. This is an important step in the learning process, as you are working to support a range of different learners in your classrooms.

Additional knowledge is gained when your team together discusses students' specific learning needs. Through collaboration, you can collectively identify ways to reach every learner.

During these focused conversations in team meetings, collective expertise is developed. Team members assimilate information from the reading and learn from each other. Adult learners benefit by engaging in a sustained inquiry and by hearing others think out loud. In so doing, teachers acquire more tools in their teacher toolbox. They are more prepared to effectively navigate future challenges.

Source 2: Modeling and Think-Alouds

"I've heard of the Numbered Heads strategy, but I don't really know how to use it. It sounds like it's for first graders," Kirsten confesses to her colleagues in the science department. Tatiana responds, "Actually, Numbered Heads Together works for all ages. It's one of my favorite strategies to use. In fact, I use it almost every week because the kids really enjoy it. They participate so much more. Sometimes they surprise me with how much they know!"

◀ DOUG SHARES HOW MODELING BUILDS TEACHER EXPERTISE
resources.corwin.com/collectiveefficacy

Numbered Heads Together is an example of a learning strategy that's not always clear in written form. Having a theoretical understanding from reading about the strategy may not be sufficient for a teacher to implement it well. It's often more beneficial when teachers are able to see an instructional strategy like Numbered Heads Together in action. Since thinking is invisible, modeling is a way that teachers can gain insight into a colleague's thinking as they watch an explicit demonstration of a concept, practice, or disposition. Effective teacher modeling includes a verbal description of how one person is breaking down a concept into manageable chunks.

An important aspect of modeling is a think-aloud. When a teacher incorporates a think-aloud into modeling, they share the reasons why they are making specific instructional choices. In these situations, metacognition, or thinking about your thinking, is increased. This may include knowledge gained from previous attempts and realizing when to make particular adjustments. Modeling helps to make the acquisition of a nuanced concept more understandable, as teachers are clued into a colleague's thinking and how that person processes information. A think-aloud is not limited to a demonstration of a strategy. In other instances, teachers may think aloud to model a disposition, such as how to analyze a piece of text or how to navigate through a conflict. Thinking aloud invites others into the teacher's mind, often offering a cognitive boost.

◀ GIULIA DISCUSSES HOW TEAM TALK FOCUSES ON STUDENT LEARNING, NOT WHAT WAS "COVERED"
resources.corwin.com/collectiveefficacy

When team members model practices, content, and dispositions, there are benefits for all participants, whether giving or receiving the think-aloud. Figure 3.12 offers a planning tool for teachers to use when developing a think-aloud. Modeling and think-alouds encourage teachers, just like students, to self-reflect, self-monitor, and self-evaluate.

FIGURE 3.12 MODELING AND THINK-ALOUD PLANNING TOOL

1. **Identify the strategy, concept, task, or disposition.**	
2. **State the purpose of the strategy, concept, task, or disposition.**	
3. **Explain how and when the strategy, concept, task, or disposition will be used.**	
4. **Use analogies to link prior knowledge to new learning.**	
5. **Demonstrate how the strategy, concept, task, or disposition is completed.**	
6. **Alert learners of errors to avoid.**	
7. **Assess the use of the strategy, concept, task, or disposition.**	

Source: Adapted from Fisher and Frey (2015).

Source 3: Role-Plays

Another aspect of input training involves creating opportunities for teachers to practice a strategy with each other before trying it with students. This may include test-driving the technique through modeling and explanations using student-friendly terms. Team members can observe the strategy from a student's point of view rather than their own, which may help them to refine their own practice. Since the team is addressing a common challenge, it makes sense that teachers have a strong understanding of anticipated challenges that may impede student learning. Role-playing can help to uncover potential hurdles. In this way, teachers can explicitly address areas that may be challenging to students.

Your team members can take turns practicing, observing, and providing each other with specific feedback that develops the expertise of each person. It's also useful to find and watch videos of teachers using the strategy if a video is available. Many videos are freely available on YouTube. The video doesn't have to be an exemplar; it can be helpful to talk through what was well done and what could be improved. This is a low-stakes way to develop understanding in a collaborative setting.

People gain knowledge and skills through repeated exposure and practice, which is necessary for adults' learning. This focused, deliberate practice results in stronger team relationships and greater student learning. At times, however, our colleagues need greater support and additional TLC to gain confidence to participate fully in collaborative professional learning experiences. In these cases, teams consider specific supports to assist colleagues. We can be proactive by anticipating challenges that may arise. Take note of potential challenges and determine ways to avoid them or move past them in Figure 3.13 on the next page.

NOTES

_____

_____

_____

_____

_____

_____

_____

_____

_____

_____

_____

_____

_____

FIGURE 3.13 PLANNING TO OVERCOME CHALLENGES

POTENTIAL CHALLENGES	HOW TO PREVENT/AVOID	HOW TO TRIAGE AND MOVE FORWARD

Now that we've discussed conditions and methods that promote professional learning, let's revisit the situation at Bayside Middle School. With updated knowledge and a shared commitment to learning at all levels, the teachers and administrators have updated how PD is determined and delivered at Bayside.

ACT 2: WORK SMARTER, NOT HARDER

It's 1:30 on a Wednesday afternoon in October, a week before progress reports are due. Bayside High School's seventh-grade English teachers, Lily, Lourdes, and Barb, are headed to the multi-purpose room for PD. While the teacher contract requires mandatory training for two hours each quarter, the Bayside Middle staff has agreed to quarterly department meetings to review student work samples, share best practices that have impacted learning, and calibrate their expectations of student performance.

Teachers at Bayside Middle are prepared for this meeting because the administrators invite teachers to provide input into each meeting's agenda, which is shared with all staff through a web-based document that everyone can access. The tables in the multi-purpose room are arranged into groups to foster teacher collaboration. Lily, Lourdes, and Barb sit at a table near the other English teachers and take out students' essays from the team's recent study of *The Book Thief* by Markus Zusak, as they are in the Building Educator Knowledge and Skills phase of a Collective Efficacy Cycle. After reviewing students' data in September, the team determined that the common challenge was students' understanding and analysis of characters and narrators' points of view in texts. The evidence-based strategy they selected for learning and implementing is modeling. Lily, Lourdes, and Barb are interested to find out if their think-alouds about narrators have been effective, as determined by what students share in their writing.

There isn't a formal start to the meeting, as it's unnecessary because all the teachers are in the multi-purpose room, collaborating. Denise is one of Bayside's vice principals and she has been working alongside the seventh-grade English teachers throughout this Collective Efficacy Cycle. As Denise pulls up a chair, Barb makes room for her to join their discussion.

MODULE 3 RECAP: WHAT DID WE LEARN?

Yay, team! You can drive school strengthening efforts by making decisions that promote students' success. You've started making plans that develop individual and collective learning. Take stock regarding your team's sense of efficacy—what specific actions occurred that brought your team closer together? Record your ideas and evidence for each indicator in Figure 3.14. Questions to consider in this reflection that center of building educator knowledge include:

- Did we review evidence-based practices?

- Did we collaboratively identify an evidence-based practice to address the common challenge?

- In what ways are we gaining professional knowledge as a team?

FIGURE 3.14 COLLECTIVE EFFICACY CYCLE REFLECTIVE QUESTIONS

QUESTION	MY THOUGHTS/DEGREE OF COLLECTIVE EFFICACY				
Mastery Experiences: In what ways was our team successful? Identify specific instances when our actions were skillful.	1	2	3	4	5
Trust: Was there a sense of trust among the team while determining the common challenge? Note instances when trust was strong.	1	2	3	4	5
Problem Solving: In what ways did we work together to solve problems? Describe when and how the team supported each other.	1	2	3	4	5
Assets-Orientation: When faced with a problem, did we maintain an assets-oriented stance? Note any situations when the team built upon students' strengths, interests, and background knowledge.	1	2	3	4	5
Efficiency: Did we adhere to agreed-upon protocols and use our time well? Write down times when our meetings felt productive.	1	2	3	4	5
Optimism: What was the general tenor/emotional tone of our meetings? Describe instances when we supported each other to maintain a positive outlook.	1	2	3	4	5

Access videos and resources for this module at
resources.corwin.com/collectiveefficacy

Module 4
COLLABORATIVE PLANNING AND SAFE PRACTICE

MODULE OVERVIEW

Now that teams have learned about an evidence-based practice, teachers have multiple opportunities to implement it with students during Safe Practice. This phase of the Collective Efficacy Cycle is considered *Safe Practice* because no one is permitted to observe teachers who are practicing the strategy. This provides assurance to teachers that coaches, principals, and district leaders will allow the teacher to experiment with the strategy without fear of being judged or evaluated.

During the two weeks of Safe Practice, teachers engage in deliberate practice of the strategy in order to deepen their expertise. Expertise does not occur simply because of an accumulation of experience. Rather, genuine expertise results from an intense focus toward a precise goal. Deliberate practice pushes us out of our comfort zone and causes our brains to form better mental models, which improves the skill we're learning. During Safe Practice, the team meets to discuss progress and troubleshoot any implementation issues that have surfaced. Safe Practice also offers teams opportunities to hone their abilities to provide evidence-based feedback. The Innovation Configuration Map in Figure 4.1 provides teams with an understanding of the ideal state of Safe Practice.

◄ INTRODUCTION TO MODULE 4
resources.corwin.com/collectiveefficacy

FIGURE 4.1 INNOVATION CONFIGURATION (IC) MAP FOR SAFE PRACTICE

1: IDEAL STATE	2: DEVELOPING	3: STARTING OUT
Each team member implements the evidence-based practice with students and meets **all** of the following criteria.	Each team member implements the evidence-based practice with students and meets **most** (50–99%) of the success criteria.	Each team member implements the evidence-based practice with students and meets **some** (0–49%) of the success criteria.

Team members

- Implement the practice three times or more

- Reflect on early results and adjusts, as necessary, to ensure student learning

- Collaboratively discuss the strategy and/or student learning three times or more

- Develop and refine the ability to provide evidence-based feedback

- Reduce or eliminate evaluative statements that impact interpersonal and intrapersonal interactions

Assumptions and evaluative statements that go unchecked can diminish the team's sense of efficacy. While teams may have established shared agreements, there are still occasions when miscommunications may puncture the learning culture and cohesiveness of the team. In the following vignette, you'll learn of a situation that causes the team to stop trusting Sangita, one of the team members. As you read, consider if you've witnessed a similar situation. We offer an updated vignette later in the module to demonstrate how the situation with Sangita could be handled more effectively.

NOTES

_____
_____
_____
_____
_____
_____
_____

ACT 1: WORK HARDER, NOT SMARTER

Sangita misses the team meeting where the group has committed to sharing student work related to the most recent Collective Efficacy Cycle. She doesn't provide an explanation but calls in sick. It may be assumed that Sangita has deliberately stayed home to avoid presenting her students' work samples. Without checking this assumption, we may begin to believe that Sangita faked being sick so that she wouldn't have to participate in the team meeting and share her students' work samples. We might then begin to question Sangita's commitment to her students and the team. This belief may bleed into other aspects of our perceptions of Sangita. We may make additional assumptions based upon the story we've concocted in our heads, even if there isn't any evidence that Sangita has shirked her responsibilities. With further unchecked assumptions, we begin to believe that Sangita is an uncaring and irresponsible person. We don't trust her anymore and avoid including her during team meetings.

While this example may seem a bit extreme, misunderstandings like this occur all the time. For a variety of reasons, we don't reach out or ask questions that might disconfirm an inference we have made. Instead, we tend to believe our assumptions, which then become our reality. Disconnects and other miscommunications may drive a wedge between colleagues or cause the whole team to spin their wheels. By tuning in and asking questions, we can avoid many of these situations. This is especially critical during peer-to-peer observations, as unchecked assumptions can get out of hand and derail the team.

SUPPORTING RISK TAKING

Educators know that students must be supported to take academic risks. They pose thought-provoking questions and challenge students to solve complex problems. Teachers prompt and encourage, providing the space for breakthrough moments to occur. We often call them "aha moments" and feel a mixture of excitement for the student and validation of our teaching when they happen. We are aware that deep learning often occurs when students' thinking and understanding stretch beyond what they currently know. We love those lightbulb moments! And just as we guide students to take academic risks, we must also be willing to apply these same ideas to ourselves as learners. Let's explore how teams can deepen their expertise of the identified evidence-based practice during Safe Practice.

THE SAFE PRACTICE PHASE

As noted in Module 3, teams select and begin engaging in activities that build their knowledge and expertise of evidence-based practice. This practice focuses on the Collective Efficacy Cycle and addresses an identified student need: the common challenge. The next phase of learning for educators involves team members implementing the evidence-based practice with students in real time. This is called Safe Practice.

During the Safe Practice phase of the Collective Efficacy Cycle, there is an understanding that teachers will not be observed or evaluated by an administrator, coach, or another district official. Protecting teachers from observations and evaluations allows the teacher to try out the evidence-based practice without the possibility of feeling judged while they learn and refine it. It's critical that Safe Practice is honored such that teachers can experiment as they take on a new approach and adjust the implementation in accordance with students' needs.

The expectation during Safe Practice is that teachers implement the strategy on multiple occasions; usually, this means three to four times per week. For example, if the team selects Reciprocal Teaching as the evidence-based practice to address student learning needs, each team member will introduce and implement it with students. There isn't an exact number of times that each teacher should implement the strategy, but we recommend at least five, depending upon the complexity of the strategy, students' needs, and their response to it. Safe Practice affords each teacher multiple opportunities to not only implement the strategy but also to determine the impact on student learning.

While in Safe Practice, which typically lasts two to three weeks, teams meet and discuss their impressions of the strategy and early results of student learning. Teams utilize this time to continue their dialogue about the strategy, refine it, and analyze how student learning is being affected and what adjustments might be necessary for even greater learning. This phase is also marked by teachers' deliberate practice toward a defined goal. In this case, the goal is for teachers to develop expertise using the identified evidence-based strategy. What sets expert teachers apart from average teachers is the quality and quantity of their deliberate practice and the analysis that results from it.

NAÏVE OR DELIBERATE PRACTICE?

It's important that teachers are aware of *how* they are practicing the evidence-based strategy, as there are two different kinds of practice: deliberate practice and naïve practice (Ericsson & Pool, 2016). *Naïve practice* occurs when a skill is repeated, and the learner accumulates experience, while *deliberate practice* is purposeful, goal oriented, involves feedback, and requires getting out of one's comfort zone. Because the point is to systematically develop expertise, let's explore the characteristics of naïve practice and deliberate practice.

Naïve practice is characterized by starting with a general idea of a skill and practicing it until we reach an acceptable level. When the skill becomes automatic, we often will put less effort because concentration is no longer needed. Think back to when you learned to drive. You likely had to concentrate the first few times behind the wheel until you became good at it and driving became routine for you. Now when you get into your car, you don't have to think. You just drive—it's automatic. And while you might have been practicing driving for the past fifteen or twenty years, your driving skills haven't improved that much. The problem with naïve practice is that accumulated experience doesn't lead to improvement, even after years of practice. People falsely believe that repetition alone will improve their performance (Ericsson & Pool, 2016).

FIGURE 4.2 NAÏVE VS. DELIBERATE PRACTICE

NAÏVE PRACTICE IS . . .	DELIBERATE PRACTICE IS . . .
• The building up of experience	• Pushing beyond your comfort zone
• Routine and automatic	• Working toward a well-defined, specific goal
• Maintaining your comfort zone	• An intense focus on practice activities
	• Marked by high-quality feedback
	• The development of a mental model of expertise

On the other hand, as noted in Figure 4.2, deliberate practice is considerably more purposeful and precise. The learner practices with intention *every time* and receives specific feedback about their progress. During Safe Practice, teachers get feedback by reflecting on their implementation of the evidence-based strategy and from students in the form of their understanding. A teacher's ability to gather implementation information and analyze it is a way to coach oneself. The key to expertise is not to attain a satisfactory skill level and to stop there. Research indicates that once a person reaches that acceptable performance and automaticity (think of the driving analogy), more "practice" of the naïve variety doesn't lead to improvement (Ericsson & Pool, 2016). Instead, expertise develops through deliberate practice and pushing yourself to be better.

PRINCIPLES OF DELIBERATE PRACTICE

Leadership guru Jim Collins asserts that "good is the enemy of great" and while he made this statement in reference to business, this is an important lesson for educators, too. Too often, people settle for "good enough." Whether it's driving, taking up a new activity, or teaching—by engaging in naïve practice, we learn enough to get by, but we seldom push ourselves to go beyond "good enough." And while "good enough" is usually sufficient for playing the piano or baking a cake, cognitive challenges, such as learning to speak a new language, playing a new musical instrument, or teaching using a new strategy, require enhanced mental training or deliberate practice.

Research across a wide range of fields indicates that experience alone doesn't improve one's proficiency.

Research across a wide range of fields indicates that experience alone doesn't improve one's proficiency. In education, it's been noted that "typical approaches to teacher preparation and professional development have produced inconsistent teacher effectiveness" (Deans for Impact, 2016, p. 3). Deans for Impact maintains that there are five principles of deliberate practice that are particularly relevant to enhancing teacher expertise; they are described in Figure 4.3, and a visual of the process is shown in Figure 4.4.

FIGURE 4.3 THE FIVE PRINCIPLES OF DELIBERATE PRACTICE

	PRINCIPLE	DESCRIPTION
1	Push beyond one's comfort zone	Teaching is challenging work and deliberate practice requires presenting challenges that push teachers just beyond their current abilities.
2	Work toward well-defined, specific goals	Deliberate practice requires teachers to set specific, measurable goals that focus on a particular aspect of teaching rather than working toward broad general improvement.
3	Focus intently on practice activities	Teachers engage in low-stakes simulations in order to rehearse a skill prior to classroom instruction.
4	Receive and respond to high-quality feedback	Focused feedback is provided immediately after a teacher practices the skill. This feedback is integrated as the teacher repeats the same skill.
5	Develop a mental model of expertise	Teachers have a clear picture of the skill that allows them to self-monitor and adjust their implementation based on student learning needs.

FIGURE 4.4 THE FIVE PRINCIPLES OF DELIBERATE PRACTICE VISUAL

PUSH BEYOND one's comfort zone

Work toward well-defined, **SPECIFIC GOALS**

FOCUS intently on practice activities

Receive and respond to **HIGH-QUALITY FEEDBACK**

Develop a **MENTAL MODEL** of expertise

Source: Deans for Impact (2016).

In any field, experts not only practice deliberately, but they also think deliberately. For example, playing chess well involves more than setting up a chessboard and moving the rooks and pawns arbitrarily. Instead, expert chess players deliberate for minutes between each move, exploring all the possibilities, thinking through the consequences of each move, and planning a sequence of moves that might follow. Much like the game of chess, teaching entails continuous thinking, analyzing, and responding.

A mental model is how you think about an idea, an object, or any other concept. An easy way to understand a mental model is by considering an image, such as the *Mona Lisa*, because many of us can picture that painting in our minds. Some people have more complex mental models of the Mona Lisa and can provide rich descriptions about her facial features and where she's sitting, while others recall fewer details. We each have mental models that are constructed by our experiences, perceptions, and understandings of the world. Deliberate practice in teaching involves developing more nuanced and sophisticated mental models of teaching and learning processes.

Teaching expertise, then, requires that teachers improve and extend the skills we already have and ensure those skills align with identified evidence-based practices identified in the Visible Learning Meta^X or What Works Clearinghouse. Use Figures 4.5 through 4.9 to consider the ways you currently practice deliberately at the individual and team levels. As with previous exercises, teams may decide to use the questions to reflect all five principles individually but select one to two principles to focus their discussions.

◄ CHRISTOPHER AND GIULIA CONFER ABOUT IMPLEMENTATION OF THE EVIDENCE-BASED PRACTICE
resources.corwin.com/collectiveefficacy

FIGURE 4.5 REFLECTIVE QUESTIONS ABOUT PRACTICING WITH PURPOSE

QUESTION	MY THOUGHTS	OUR COLLECTIVE THOUGHTS
In what ways does our team jointly create challenges that push novice and veteran teachers outside their comfort zones?		
In what ways do we support each other when learning a challenging skill?		

FIGURE 4.6 REFLECTIVE QUESTIONS ABOUT DEFINING A SPECIFIC GOAL

QUESTION	MY THOUGHTS	OUR COLLECTIVE THOUGHTS
Are clear and specific goals jointly created and agreed on by each team member of our team?		
In what ways are we providing specific, actionable feedback related to the goal?		

FIGURE 4.7 REFLECTIVE QUESTIONS ABOUT EXTENDED PRACTICE OPPORTUNITIES

QUESTION	MY THOUGHTS	OUR COLLECTIVE THOUGHTS
In what ways are we providing time outside of the classroom for additional opportunities to hone a particular skill?		
Is sufficient time afforded for extended practice?		

FIGURE 4.8   REFLECTIVE QUESTIONS ABOUT RESPONDING TO FEEDBACK

QUESTION	MY THOUGHTS	OUR COLLECTIVE THOUGHTS
Does each member of our team agree upon and use common language and structures for feedback?		
Is feedback focused on specific, agreed-upon goals?		

FIGURE 4.9   REFLECTIVE QUESTIONS ABOUT DEVELOPING MENTAL MODELS

QUESTION	MY THOUGHTS	OUR COLLECTIVE THOUGHTS
What processes are in place for us to self-monitor whether our student learning has increased?		
In what ways do we compare our ideas of student learning with evidence of student learning?		

Everyone has and uses mental models. What sets expert teachers apart from others is the quality and quantity of their mental models. Through deliberate practice, expert teachers develop highly complex and sophisticated mental models that allow them to make "faster, more accurate decisions and respond more quickly and effectively in a given situation" (Ericsson & Pool, 2016, p. 62). In other words, experts see the forest when everyone else only sees the trees.

EDUCATOR AGENCY

Deliberate practice is often empowering to individuals and teams, especially when teachers' efforts are validated by evidence of student learning. A Collective Efficacy Cycle offers one such way to further teacher learning and expertise while commending teachers for their efforts. Whether you are a coach, district leader, principal, or teacher, the feedback educators give to each other can fuel self-efficacy and teacher collective efficacy. Fisher and Frey (2021) suggest using this simple formula: "When you did x, then y occurred" (p. 77). Outcome-oriented statements that follow this formula link educators' efforts with their impact on students. Implying that teachers should work harder, longer, or faster does little to inspire the collegiality, connection, and hope that teachers crave.

◄ DOUG SHARES ABOUT DEVELOPING EDUCATOR AGENCY
resources.corwin.com/collectiveefficacy

Teams can further own their professional growth when their agency and voice are affirmed by their schools and districts. Agency at the team level involves teachers' capacity "to act purposefully and constructively to direct their own professional growth and contribute to the growth of colleagues" (Calvert, 2016, p. 4). In other words, optimal learning occurs when people are actively engaged and receive growth-producing feedback. On the flip side, learning may be reduced if unproductive praise is piled on or the learner feels judged.

UNPRODUCTIVE PRAISE

Though statements of praise to colleagues, such as "I loved that" and "That's awesome!" are meant to be kind, these messages are both evaluative and vague. Although praise is natural and is woven into the fabric of our society, if we don't mention *why* something was awesome, or, to be more accurate with teaching and learning, why something was *effective*, we're not providing feedback that could reinforce specific teaching behaviors. The message here is not to stop praising others; instead, it's to encourage you to link your praise to a colleague's instructional move and the resulting impact on students.

Experts see the forest when everyone else only sees the trees.

Additionally, it's important to be aware of when praise is being provided. It can be both demeaning and unproductive if a colleague is praised for relatively trivial achievements. For example, "You got to the meeting on time today. Great job," conveys a message of low expectations or sarcasm. Alternatively, we can look for opportunities to fortify our colleagues' intrinsic motivation by providing sincere feedback that highlights and validates specific behavioral actions and elements of a task well-done. Leadership guru Ken Blanchard (2009) reminds us that "feedback is the breakfast of champions." Feedback that is grounded in specific points reduces bias and judgment during interpersonal communications.

NONJUDGMENTAL REFLECTION

Judgment is the process of forming an opinion or reaching a conclusion based upon available information. Judgment occurs from the thoughts we have and in the meaning we attach to them. Negative thoughts such as anger, anxiety, and sadness occur when we judge others, and ourselves, too harshly. Use Figure 4.10 to think about your own experiences with judgment.

Optimal learning occurs when people are actively engaged and receive growth-producing feedback.

FIGURE 4.10 A MINDFUL MOMENT

Have you felt judged in your professional career? If so, by who? How did you feel, and what were the circumstances? What could have made that situation better?

To manage judgment of ourselves and others, we can develop a habit of reframing a negative, critical thought into a nonjudgmental version. Increasing our awareness of judgmental thinking can be daunting, as we may learn that we have many critical thoughts on any given day. We each have an inner critic, and it can be helpful to understand how to manage these thoughts.

Learning to reframe negative thoughts helps us to provide feedback in nonjudgmental ways to ourselves and others. Both *what* we say and *how* we say it matter. Judgmental thoughts negatively affect our feelings of self-worth and can also damage relationships with others. Reframing is a useful tool to enhance problem solving and resolve conflicts, and it can even reduce feelings of burnout and overwhelm (Czach, 2020). Jot down some judgmental thoughts in Figure 4.11 and reframe them into nonjudgmental versions. There are a few examples to get you started.

FIGURE 4.11 REFRAMING JUDGMENTAL THOUGHTS

JUDGMENTAL THOUGHT	REFRAMED NONJUDGMENTAL THOUGHT
I'm overwhelmed. I can't do it.	When we're pressed for time, and I'm stressed and tired, I tend to lose my temper quickly.
She stays calm and I always feel like a wreck.	I admire her ability to stay calm and would like to learn how to do this for myself.
He calls in sick all the time.	Is there another way of thinking about this? Perhaps he's sick because he's under a lot of pressure that I'm not aware of.

OBSERVATION OR EVALUATION?

Additionally, we live in a culture of evaluations and judgments. Our language is peppered with comparative and evaluative terms that cause others to feel judged, such as *faster, thinner, prettier, better,* and *smarter.* Evaluative statements can cause problems in our interpersonal relationships because when we judge someone or their circumstances, we are using our own unique lens that is shaped by our beliefs, experiences, assumptions, and expectations. Our perceptions may not be accurate, and we risk offending others or causing them to shut down. If our words cause someone to armor up, it's unlikely that the intended message is received.

When our perceptions are articulated and framed as an evaluation of another person or their situation, we imply that something is wrong with them. Comments perceived as judgments or criticism can lead to defensiveness, resistance, and disconnection in the relationship. Instead, communication is more effective when evaluation is separated from observation.

An observation is different than an evaluation because an observation is objective. An objective statement is descriptive and provides just the facts, not one's interpretation of the facts, or evaluation of whether the facts are good or bad. It consists of noticing concrete things and actions. Figure 4.12 provides examples of evaluation and observation.

◀ **OBSERVATION OR EVALUATION?**
resources.corwin.com/collectiveefficacy

FIGURE 4.12 EXAMPLES OF THE DIFFERENCES BETWEEN EVALUATION AND OBSERVATION STATEMENTS

EVALUATION (Subjective, Interpretation Based Upon Assumptions)	OBSERVATION (Objective, Just the Facts)
That parent is ignoring me because I emailed them last week and they haven't gotten back to me.	It's been five days since I sent an email. There hasn't been a response yet.
I can't rely on Julio because he's always late.	Julio arrived 10 minutes late to the meeting this morning.
My friend doesn't care about me. He didn't say anything about my birthday.	It was my birthday yesterday, and I didn't hear from my friend.

How many times have you made an inaccurate judgment or acted upon an assumption that turned out to be incorrect? It happens all the time, so it behooves us to be diligent to avoid misunderstandings. The ability to describe practice without judgment may be counterintuitive because giving compliments ("I liked how you . . .") is a part of our social contract. And since teachers are rarely outside their own classrooms, they've had fewer opportunities to practice gathering evidence and describing it in nonjudgmental ways, but this skill can be learned. Description of this sort is based upon judgment-free evidence. We can think about it as describing what is seen, not judging what *you think about* what is seen.

As we'll learn in Module 5, peer observations focus on the *improvement* of practice, not the *evaluation* of practice. When we observe teaching and learning, descriptive statements help teachers and teacher teams to determine cause-and-effect relationships. In other words, in what ways did the teacher's instruction cause students to learn? Use the exercise in Figure 4.13 to collaborate with your team and hone your ability to distinguish between objective and subjective statements.

FIGURE 4.13   DISTINGUISH BETWEEN EVALUATION AND OBSERVATION

STATEMENT	EVALUATION OR OBSERVATION?
"You always take too long."	
"You called on six girls during this section of the lesson."	
"Gary didn't ask for my opinion during the meeting."	
"If you were better at planning, this wouldn't have happened."	
"Students took 9 minutes to get settled."	

Think of it this way: if a doctor tells the patient they're healthy without taking any vital signs, you wonder how the doctor made that determination. Similarly, if a home inspector says your house looks sturdy without examining the slab or walls, you question their credibility. It's the same way with teaching. If we use our assumptions to determine what's good or bad, we are unlikely to understand the causal relationship between teaching and learning. The evidence needed for examination of practices is found in the nooks and crannies of instruction, the classroom context, and student learning. Holding an evidence-based debriefing from a more visible starting point surfaces richer conversation than debating individual beliefs and assumptions.

THE LADDER OF INFERENCE

Once we learn how to provide descriptive evidence, it can still be challenging to remain in the judgment-free zone. Most of us have a tendency, consciously or unconsciously, to default back to making assumptions based on our own experiences. In addition to making assumptions, we are also prone to comparing ourselves to others, which is also a form of judgment. This habit keeps us from being evidence based and bias free during peer-to-peer observations.

A tool that can be helpful for staying in the descriptive zone is the Ladder of Inference. The ladder is a visual image and provides language to keep you from making unfounded assumptions. The bottom rung of the ladder represents facts. This is directly observable evidence and where we strive to operate when we make peer-to-peer observations. As you move up the ladder, you get farther from the evidence and closer to your own assumptions, conclusions, and beliefs. Figure 4.14 provides an infographic to help individuals and teams to remain vigilant when collecting evidence-based and bias-

◄ CHRISTOPHER DISCUSSES THE LADDER OF INFERENCE
resources.corwin.com/collectiveefficacy

free data during classroom observations, and Figure 4.15 offers a space for reflection. The Ladder of Inference tool can also be used to improve interpersonal and intrapersonal interactions.

NOTES

_____

_____

_____

_____

_____

_____

_____

_____

FIGURE 4.14 THE LADDER OF INFERENCE

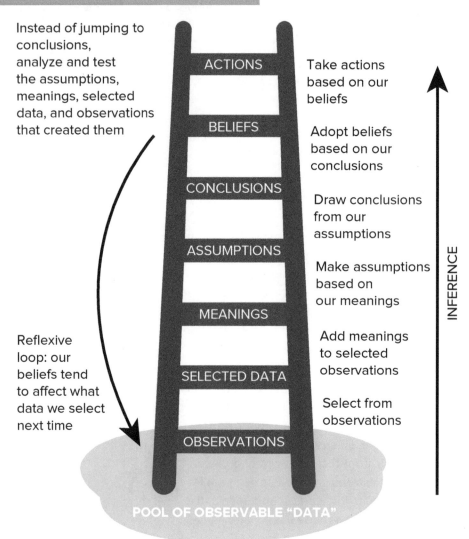

Instead of jumping to conclusions, analyze and test the assumptions, meanings, selected data, and observations that created them

Reflexive loop: our beliefs tend to affect what data we select next time

ACTIONS — Take actions based on our beliefs

BELIEFS — Adopt beliefs based on our conclusions

CONCLUSIONS — Draw conclusions from our assumptions

ASSUMPTIONS — Make assumptions based on our meanings

MEANINGS — Add meanings to selected observations

SELECTED DATA — Select from observations

OBSERVATIONS

INFERENCE

POOL OF OBSERVABLE "DATA"

Source: Wikimedia Commons. Model developed by Chris Argyris.

NOTES

FIGURE 4.15   A MINDFUL MOMENT

Identify two ways that the Ladder of Inference tool can assist you in your personal and professional relationships.

1.

2.

Earlier in the module, we introduced you to a situation where a team made assumptions about a colleague. In that vignette, Sangita was ostracized because the team wrongfully assumed that Sangita was not committed to the team or her students because she was absent from a team meeting. Judgments were made that led to harsh conclusions. In the following vignette, the team doesn't make assumptions and instead inquires with compassion about Sangita's absence from the meeting. As you read, consider how the Ladder of Inference suggested in Figure 4.14 offers people a way to consider the observational evidence before assigning meaning and forming conclusions.

ACT 2: WORK SMARTER, NOT HARDER

Sangita misses the team meeting where the group has committed to sharing student work samples related to the most recent Collective Efficacy Cycle. She doesn't provide an explanation but calls in sick. Rather than assume that Sangita has shirked her commitments and stayed home to avoid presenting her students' work samples, we are compassionate and believe that there must be a good reason as to why Sangita hasn't communicated with the team. Instead of making judgments about Sangita's commitment to her students and the team, we reach out to Sangita out of a sense of care for our team member. Without prying into Sangita's personal business, we call her to express our concern and help should she need anything. Sangita responds, "Thank you so much for calling. Someone broke into our house and robbed us while we were out walking last night. They took our computers and laptops. They went through all of my things and stole my jewelry. The worst part is that my pictures and videos of my kids are gone, along with the strand of pearls my grandmother left me when she passed. I've just been so sick about this, and I couldn't sleep a wink last night. I'm sorry I didn't call. The police asked me to make a list of everything that was stolen . . . and it's just really hard, you know?"

Without attention to the interpersonal dynamics, teams may spiral into dysfunction.

This version of the vignette reminds us that actions may be motivated by good reasons. We can minimize miscommunications by checking our assumptions and maintaining a compassionate stance. Without attention to the interpersonal dynamics, teams may spiral into dysfunction, which diminishes the learning culture and threatens the trust the team needs to fully participate and benefit from Safe Practice.

The Safe Practice phase of the Collective Efficacy Cycle is designed so teachers have both opportunities and an environment that promotes the deliberate practice of an evidence-based practice. There are certainly times for naïve practice in our lives, such as during recreational sports and other activities where we just want to have fun. However, teams will be unlikely to cultivate collective teacher efficacy without deliberate practice. Deliberate practice requires the learner to get out of their comfort zone, because there is challenge and struggle when you push yourself out of your comfort zone. Without doing so, you'll never improve.

MODULE 4 RECAP: WHAT DID WE LEARN?

Yay, team! You engaged in two to three weeks of Safe Practice, implementing the evidence-based practice multiple times in a low-stakes environment. While teachers practice deliberately in order to learn and refine this practice, the team also meets to discuss progress and problem-solve any issues that surfaced during implementation. This phase of the Collective Efficacy Cycle also offers teams opportunities to hone their skills in making judgment-free statements before making peer observations. The following questions can support teams' reflections on generating collective teacher efficacy throughout Safe Practice. Talent wins games, but teamwork wins championships.

- Did we discuss and share agreements about observations and evaluations?
- Did we collaboratively discuss how we might use the Ladder of Inference to move our team's learning forward?
- In what ways are we practicing deliberately and gaining professional knowledge as a team?

NOTES

_____

_____

_____

_____

_____

_____

_____

_____

_____

_____

_____

_____

_____

_____

_____

_____

_____

_____

_____

_____

FIGURE 4.16 COLLECTIVE EFFICACY CYCLE REFLECTIVE QUESTIONS

QUESTION	MY THOUGHTS/DEGREE OF COLLECTIVE EFFICACY				
Mastery Experiences: In what ways was our team successful? Identify specific instances when our actions were skillful.	1	2	3	4	5
Trust: Was there a sense of trust among the team while determining the common challenge? Note instances when trust was strong.	1	2	3	4	5
Problem Solving: In what ways did we work together to solve problems? Describe when and how the team supported each other.	1	2	3	4	5
Assets-Orientation: When faced with a problem, did we maintain an assets-oriented stance? Note any situations when the team built upon students' strengths, interests, and background knowledge.	1	2	3	4	5
Efficiency: Did we adhere to agreed-upon protocols and use our time well? Write down times when our meetings felt productive.	1	2	3	4	5
Optimism: What was the general tenor/emotional tone of our meetings? Describe instances when we supported each other to maintain a positive outlook.	1	2	3	4	5

online resources

Access videos and resources for this module at
resources.corwin.com/collectiveefficacy

Module 5
COLLABORATIVE PLANNING AND OPENING UP PRACTICE

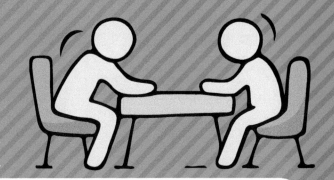

MODULE OVERVIEW

Following Safe Practice of the evidence-based strategy, educators further their individual and collective capacity through peer-to-peer observations in each other's classrooms as well as through inviting coaches and leaders into classrooms for feedback. This is a non-evaluative opportunity for us to learn from one another, as we benefit both from being observed and being the observer. The reflections that occur following peer observations are where breakthrough results are seen because conversations shift from talking about *teaching* (*what I did*) to talking about *learning* (*my impact on students*). Opening up practice through peer observations is the third specific action our teams take to systematically cultivate collective teacher efficacy.

◄ **INTRODUCTION TO MODULE 5**
resources.corwin.com/collectiveefficacy

The three major components of a peer observation are a pre-conference, an observation, and a post-conference. Each component is carefully planned to ensure that the educator being observed feels comfortable and the observers provide growth-producing, nonjudgmental feedback. During observations, observers gain insights that enhance their own practice and support the educator's effectiveness by bringing awareness of classroom contexts that may otherwise be unseen. The Innovation Configuration Map displayed in Figure 5.1 provides a description of what the ideal implementation of a peer observation process looks like as teams work through this phase of the Collective Efficacy Cycle.

◄ **PEER OBSERVATIONS AND COACHING**
resources.corwin.com/collectiveefficacy

FIGURE 5.1 INNOVATION CONFIGURATION (IC) MAP FOR PEER OBSERVATION PROCESS

1: IDEAL STATE	2: DEVELOPING	3: STARTING OUT
Each team member actively participates in a peer-to-peer observation process to deepen understanding of the evidence-based practice and meets **all** of the following criteria.	Each team member actively participates in a peer-to-peer observation process to deepen understanding of the evidence-based practice by meeting **most** (50–99%) of the success criteria.	Each team member actively participates in a peer-to-peer observation process to deepen understanding of the evidence-based practice by meeting **some** (0–49%) of the success criteria.

- Each team member observes one or more colleagues implementing the strategy
- Each team member is observed by one or more colleagues
- The team provides mentoring and coaching
- Feedback about student learning and/or implementation is provided to each educator being observed
- Feedback about mentoring is provided to the observer
- Discussion and reflection centers on the impact of student learning as a result of the evidence-based strategy

OPENING CLASSROOM DOORS AND INVITING FEEDBACK

Historically, teaching has largely been a private endeavor. While this approach promotes autonomy, many opportunities for validation and growth are missed because classroom doors are shut to colleagues. Peer observation is a way for teachers and educators to de-privatize their practice by inviting a colleague to observe a segment of a lesson. A whole lesson could be observed, but this can be a logistical challenge. Instead, a 10- to 15-minute observation of the evidence-based practice being implemented with students is sufficient for both educators to learn from each other.

ACT 1: WORK HARDER, NOT SMARTER

Kara, a new tenth-grade biology teacher at Hyatt High, hasn't participated in any type of peer observation before. She's nervous about it because she was evaluated by the administrator at her previous site and expects the peer observation step of the Collective Efficacy Cycle to be a similar experience where she'll feel judged. Kara also feels concerned that her new colleagues might think less of her if they observed in her classroom, especially during third period. She's new to this team, after all, and she wants her science department colleagues Joy and Jason to see her as an equal.

The thought of having colleagues observe in her class stresses out Kara, but she doesn't articulate this fear to anyone. Instead, she secretly hopes there's a scheduling problem or other unforeseen issue that will prevent the peer observation from actually happening. Kara tells herself that there's just too much other stuff going on right now.

Observations involve each team member being observed and observing (see Figure 5.2). We shouldn't worry that our amount of experience may preclude our ability to provide coaching and support to peers. A new teacher, or any teacher for that matter, doesn't have to have all the answers, nor should they. Instead, it works best when we ask questions that mediate others' thinking by helping them to unpack what it is they already know. Through careful preparation, each educator poses questions that cause colleagues to generate enhanced thinking that solves their own problems. All educators, even those new to the profession, can ask reflective questions, provide insights, and supply useful feedback that improves practice.

> **Many opportunities for validation and growth are missed because classroom doors are shut to colleagues.**

FIGURE 5.2   WHAT IS PEER OBSERVATION?

PEER OBSERVATION IS . . .	PEER OBSERVATION ISN'T . . .
• Structured	• Unstructured
• Focused on a single element selected by the teacher being observed	• Unscheduled
• Observing each other's practice	• About making judgments
• Learning with and from a colleague	• Evaluative
• Sharing best practices	• Shared with a principal or used for evaluation purposes
• Factual	

THE THREE COMPONENTS OF PEER OBSERVATIONS

Peer observations involve educators observing each other's practice and providing feedback that refines their instructional practices and improves students' learning. The purpose is to engage with colleagues in a job-embedded, collaborative professional learning experience in real time. The observation itself is one-third of the equation, as a pre-observation conference and post-observation conference structure are required. There is an emphasis on reflection and feedback on instruction that results in greater student learning. In this way, planning, instruction, and reflective processes are made visible to teams. The structure of a peer-to-peer observation has three components:

> **A new teacher, or any teacher for that matter, doesn't have to have all the answers, nor should they.**

1. Pre-conference observation

2. Observation

3. Post-observation conference

Careful planning of all three components of the peer observation process is crucial to its success. Your team should collaboratively discuss and set ground rules before the process begins. Ground rules may include a defined amount of time that you will observe, such as allotting 10 to 15 minutes per peer observation. Teams may also find it useful to decide how to handle challenges that arise in advance of observation cycles. For instance, following an observation, a teacher might perseverate on a thought such as, "If you had just come in 10 minutes ago, the kids were _____." Instead, a ground rule can be established that observation feedback will only address what was directly observed. Adhering to an established ground rule, such as "No excuses, just the facts," may prevent conversations between your team members from spiraling in nonproductive ways.

Another essential planning element is allowing teachers to make choices. Successful peer observations are more likely when teachers have control of the timing. Teachers working in peer observation cycles often get creative to find time in their schedules to observe and be observed. For example, some teachers have an open planning period. Others use 10 minutes while their students are in the library with another credentialed teacher. Being creative reduces the need for substitutes and minimizes other scheduling challenges.

In addition to teachers scheduling their observations, it's also beneficial for teachers to decide who is observing, who is being observed, and the related logistics. Since there's a degree of vulnerability that comes with opening up practice, it's important that the teacher being observed is comfortable with the peer who will observe. In addition, there needs to be a discussion about if and how the observing teacher will take notes. Decisions about feedback and how information is conveyed to each other could involve designing or selecting forms that are collaboratively decided upon. It's useful to ask in advance how another colleague prefers to receive feedback. Having input into this process builds trust and credibility, especially when the person observing adheres to the team's ground rules and honors the wishes of the teacher who is being observed.

HOW DOES A PEER OBSERVATION WORK?

A defining aspect of peer observations is the educator being observed leads the process and co-determines the logistics with the teacher who will observe during the pre-conference. An observation is a vehicle for professional growth, not a performance evaluation, and the teacher being observed should feel confident about every step in the process. Because the process has been co-designed, there should not be any surprises for either person. The observation centers on the evidence-based practice the team selected and implemented during Safe Practice. Through self-reflection and feedback from the observation, both teachers enhance their effectiveness and impact on students.

Because teaching is complex, it's essential that we regularly reflect on how student learning has increased as a result of our instruction. It's not sufficient to believe that if we "taught it, they got it." Instead, successful educators collaborate with peers and students about conceptions of progress and impact (Hattie & Zierer, 2017). This means reflecting on what occurs in our classrooms each day, not at the end of the year or when a summative assessment is released. The first step of reflection is self-awareness, which is often deepened through dialogue with others. Thoughtfully posed questions by a trusted colleague often trigger thinking that may not have occurred without a thinking partner.

it's important that the teacher being observed is comfortable with the peer who will observe.

The insights gleaned from the peer observation process have the potential to transform learning for both teachers and students. This is because when engaged in peer observations, we are in the driver's seat. We are directing our own learning in ways that are meaningful to us, while often solving problems that are occurring in our classrooms. Effective peer observations are job-embedded professional learning opportunities that support problem solving, the sharing of ideas, and contribute to building collective teacher efficacy.

◄ GIULIA AND BEVERLY DISCUSS THE BENEFITS OF PEER OBSERVATION
resources.corwin.com/collectiveefficacy

THE PRE-CONFERENCE OBSERVATION

The criteria for observation are determined during a pre-conference that occurs prior to the observation. The educator being observed identifies the aspect of the evidence-based practice they would like feedback about from the observer. The coach agrees to focus and provide feedback only on the area the educator has identified, not on other things happening or not happening in the classroom. This shared agreement of the expectations lowers the stress of the volunteer educator.

The teacher being observed also determines the day and time of the observation, as it is not necessary for the coach to observe an entire lesson; it may be that the volunteer educator wants feedback about their modeling or the guided practice component of the lesson. There is also discussion about when the observer will enter the classroom, for how long they will observe, and where they will be positioned. Will the observer sit in the back? In the front? Should the observer interact with students? Each of these questions is discussed and agreed upon prior to the observation.

Since understanding the implementation of an evidence-based strategy on student learning is the point of the observation, it's important the observer and teacher being observed jointly determine how this information will be captured and recorded. Will the observer take notes on a laptop or a notebook? Will the coach script what the volunteer teacher says? Will the coach take note of student responses? Will the coach ask questions of students? Again, the person being observed leads these decisions because they are putting themselves, and their practice, on display. Giving the reins to the teacher being observed and allowing them to be the driver often eliminates some of the nervousness that may accompany an observation.

◄ SCHEDULING A PEER OBSERVATION
resources.corwin.com/collectiveefficacy

Another important point to discuss during the pre-observation conference is the type and scope of feedback the volunteer teacher prefers. It's crucial that the coach listens to the volunteer teacher so they can capture this information and provide it to the volunteer teacher in a way that will be received. For instance, a volunteer teacher may ask that the coach provide feedback verbally, or perhaps visual notes will be more useful to the volunteer teacher. Again, the teacher being observed calls the shots. Both teachers can prepare for this conference by considering the questions in Figure 5.3. At the conclusion of the pre-conference, there are shared agreements and expectations between the teacher being observed and the observer.

FIGURE 5.3   PRE-OBSERVATION CONFERENCE SAMPLE QUESTIONS

LOGISTICS

The agreed observation focus is:	
The scheduled date and time is:	

PERSONAL FEELINGS

What do you hope to learn from this experience?	
How are you feeling about presenting this?	

LEARNING CONSIDERATIONS

What are your learning intentions? What are indicators of success?	
What knowledge do students already have? What other assets do they have?	

What are the student demographics?	
What might be challenging during your lesson?	
How might this challenge be overcome?	

How would you like data to be collected and organized?	
How would you like the data to be shared with you during the post-conference?	

PEER OBSERVATION PROCESS

Have you participated in a peer observation in the past? What worked well? What could have been more effective?	
Where would you like me to sit/stand when I enter the room?	
Would you like me to interact with students? If so, what is the purpose for these interactions?	

POST-OBSERVATION CONFERENCE

When will we meet to discuss the observation?	

Using an Observation Tool to Capture Evidence

An observation tool for capturing notes is also agreed upon during the pre-conference. The tool can be collaboratively developed from scratch or selected/modified from an outside source—either way works. The observer can present some different options as a starting point for the discussion and selection of a tool, but the teacher being observed makes the final decision. Some observation partners use blank paper or word-processing document, allowing writing to be free form. Others prefer to record verbatim what students say. The most important aspect of the tool is that it helps the observer to collect information that the teacher being observed has asked for.

◄ THE TEAM MONITORS STUDENT LEARNING AND RESPONDS TO NEEDS
resources.corwin.com/collectiveefficacy

THE OBSERVATION

On the scheduled date and time, the observer arrives at the classroom of the teacher being observed. It's important that the observer arrives on time and adheres to each of the agreements made during the pre-conference. During the observation, the observer only captures notes about the agreed-upon area of focus. Since there's so much going on in a classroom at any given moment, it's unfair to comment on anything else.

The first step of reflection is self-awareness, which is often deepened through dialogue with others.

Often, the first thing we discover when observing a peer is that we have very different ideas about what constitutes good practice. Frequently, our first instinct is to look for what's good—this is judgment. As we learned in Module 4, judgments can be detrimental to a relationship, so a commitment to noticing the facts is essential to the peer observation process. Recording neutral descriptions of the facts minimizes the chances of making unqualified assumptions. When the observation time is over, the observer quietly leaves the classroom. Feedback is not provided until the post-observation conference.

THE POST-OBSERVATION CONFERENCE

The pair meets to debrief the lesson according to the schedule decided during the pre-conference. Depending upon the lesson and age group, some teachers bring student work samples to discuss during the post-conference. The observer may choose to use the questions in Figure 5.4 to support this discussion, but it's important the observer listens more than talks. The value-add comes from the teacher's reflection of the lesson. The observer should resist the urge to offer advice and instead pose questions that help the peer to process out loud and unpack their thinking about the evidence-based strategy.

During the post-observation conference, the observer also presents the data captured during the observation. Along with their own observation, this information assists the teacher who was observed to consider the effectiveness of their implementation of the evidence-based strategy. By doing so, both teachers deepen their understanding of the evidence-based practice and how students are responding to it.

Providing teachers with the opportunity to share surprising moments, accomplishments, and struggles from the lesson assists them to determine next steps. Through reflection, teachers are more likely to set goals for themselves and are more vested to make improvements because they're in charge of those decisions.

Reflection about our practice helps us to process our experiences in ways that promote deeper thinking and learning. By doing so, we expand our frame of reference beyond individual lessons. Consider the questions in Figure 5.4 when planning for the post-observation conference.

FIGURE 5.4   SAMPLE POST-OBSERVATION COACHING QUESTIONS

PURPOSE	QUESTION SAMPLES
Pedagogy	• Was the evidence-based practice successful? How do you know? • In what ways did you check for understanding throughout the lesson? • What did you notice about the effectiveness of the strategies you used? • In what ways were students kept engaged? • As you reflect on this lesson, what did you consider as you differentiated?
Content	• How did you determine what students needed to know in order to be successful? • What are some of the essential questions that guided this lesson? • How did you make decisions about sequencing this lesson?
Collegial interactions	• What might some of your colleagues say about this lesson? • In what ways did interactions with colleagues support you with this lesson?
Planning	• When you planned the lesson, what were some of the criteria you considered to promote higher-order thinking? • What decisions did you make about how to monitor and adjust? • As you reflect on this lesson, how did it compare to what you planned?
Students	• When you planned the lesson, what were some of the predictions you made about students' prior knowledge? • What did you notice about students' understanding throughout the lesson? • In what ways did your understanding of students' cultural assets influence your planning?

◄ LEARNING WALKS
AND GHOST WALKS
resources.corwin.com/collectiveefficacy

Enhanced reflection occurs when the feedback provided matches the teacher's expectations from the pre-conference. This also deepens trust and increases the chances for future collaborations. Peer observations invite teachers to identify and act on goals for themselves. In this way, teachers direct their own learning. Another form of collaborative learning occurs during a learning walk and ghost walk.

LEARNING WALKS

A commitment to noticing the facts is essential to the peer observation process.

Participating in a learning walk can be a low-stakes way to experience collaborative learning. Sometimes called a walkthrough or instructional rounds, a learning walk provides opportunities for teachers to deepen their knowledge by visiting their colleagues' classrooms as a team. The focus of learning walks is to understand the degree of student learning that is occurring based upon the implementation of the evidence-based strategy. It can feel overwhelming to teachers if they believe they will be judged about everything occurring, or not occurring, in their classrooms. We can alleviate many of these fears by committing to understanding what students are *learning,* not what teachers are necessarily doing, during learning walks.

Though many teachers are familiar with learning walks that are conducted by their administrators, it's important that teams who wish to participate in learning walks collaborate and agree upon the purpose in advance of the visit. In a Collective Efficacy Cycle, the purpose for a learning walk is usually driven by the common challenge and evidence-based practice your team has selected. Learning walks are scheduled, so there are no surprise visits. Again, the idea is to learn from each other, not to nitpick or find fault with our colleagues.

Guidelines for visitors can also prevent misunderstandings from occurring. These are shared agreements that provide the emotional safety for us to take a professional risk by opening up our classrooms for colleagues to visit. The learning walk may occur during the school day, when students are present, or it can occur after school (more about that in the next section). There are advantages and disadvantages to both approaches. For example, if a learning walk occurs after school, teachers may opt to focus on an aspect of the environment, such as anchor charts that are posted or language frames that students use. If a learning walk occurs during the day, there are opportunities to observe the teacher in action and ask students questions. The following scenario gives you a look into how a group of kindergarten teachers thoughtfully structured a learning walk so they could learn from each other.

When the kindergarten team at Avalon Elementary neared the end of their Collective Efficacy Cycle, they scheduled time to engage in a learning walk with a specific focus of looking at student work in math. Prior to the learning walk, the teachers met and confirmed the learning intentions and focus of the visit: the observation of students using marbles to develop 1:1 correspondence between objects and numbers and making sense of a word problem. The problem students would be working through read:

Task: Hamid has four black marbles and three white marbles. Draw the marbles here. Josiah has five black marbles and one black marble. Draw the marbles here. Hamid thinks he has more marbles than Josiah. Is he right or wrong? How do you know? Show your thinking with the pictures, words, and numbers.

The team, having already anticipated possible student misconceptions during the lesson, referred to these notes so they were familiar prior to the learning walk:

We anticipate most students can

- Line up marbles to show 1:1 correspondence
- Write numerals for each group
- Count each side
- Write a number sentence

We anticipate these possible misconceptions:

- Thinking Josiah has more marbles because they are darker
- Not thinking of associating marbles with written numbers
- Not understanding the word *more*
- Not understanding the word *equal*
- Miscounting

Reviewing these notes prior to the learning walk reminded each member of the kindergarten team of the lesson's learning intentions—what they should be looking for. It wouldn't be fair if team members commented on other aspects of the classroom other than what was agreed upon prior to the learning walk. This focus, then, provided uniform "look-for's" about student learning for those participating in the learning walk, so the host teacher could focus on teaching the established math learning intentions.

Peer observations invite teachers to identify and act on goals for themselves.

Another important aspect that must be discussed before embarking on a learning walk is scheduling. When will the learning walk be conducted? There must be agreement as to when this will occur. What other logistics might the team consider? Other questions that should be discussed in advance of the learning walk include

- How and what information and data will be collected during the observation?
- Will observers bring clipboards or devices and record their noticings and wonderings while they are in the classroom? Will this be recorded verbatim or in shorthand?

- Will observers watch for a prescribed amount of time but record their observations outside of the classroom?
- What type of data collection tool will observers use?
- Will observers interact with students? If so, how?
- Will observers ask any or all of the three Teacher Clarity questions? If so, how will students be selected? How many will be selected?

Discussing and coming to an agreement regarding each of these questions in advance of a learning walk minimizes anxiety on the part of the host teacher because parameters for observation are agreed to in advance. There is a higher likelihood that the observation will be effective and successful for everyone involved.

Learning walks are not limited to those in the same grade level; there are many ways your team can design learning walks. It is often helpful for teams to design learning walks where they can visit the grade levels that come before and after theirs, such as fourth-grade teachers visiting third- and fifth-grade classrooms. Besides increasing cohesion across the school site, these vertical learning walks provide us with enhanced understandings of students' capabilities and developmental stages. Information learned from vertical learning walks often assists teams to craft their next steps and ensure students are appropriately prepared for the next grade level. Focusing on how and what students are learning in colleagues' classrooms helps us better deliver instruction to our students.

Participating in a learning walk can be a low-stakes way to experience collaborative learning.

Another benefit of teachers engaging in learning walks is that they can be more rapid-fire than whole school instructional rounds or walk-throughs. Teacher teams identify short times in their schedules when they are available to make visits to other classrooms or open their doors to colleagues. This is often less cumbersome to manage because fewer people need to coordinate schedules. Teachers often appreciate being empowered and trusted with these responsibilities by their administrators; allowing teachers to determine their own schedules is a small gesture that reaps lots of rewards.

At the end of each learning walk, there is designated time for observers to sift through their notes to provide feedback to the host teacher, as well as frame one to two questions they have in the form of wonderings. Wonderings are a less threatening method of asking probing questions when an observer wants to get additional information. This provides another layer of emotional safety to the host teacher. Learning walks are an essential aspect of professional learning. It's job-embedded, differentiated learning that engages us to improve instructional effectiveness in ways that are useful and relevant. There is a greater likelihood that teachers will apply understandings and insights gained through learning walks into their classroom practice than what they might get through traditional "sit-and-get" professional development. Another method for understanding student learning occurs through ghost walks.

GHOST WALKS

Ghost walks, like learning walks, are also scheduled. They don't happen haphazardly or on a whim. However, ghost walks occur when students are not present in the classroom, which is often a great way for teams to begin opening up their practice. Some teams elect to conduct ghost walks during a free prep period, at lunch, or after school. One of the advantages of participating in a ghost walk is that teachers can focus on the classroom environment since there aren't any students in the room. Similar to learning walks, it's important that ghost walks are structured and don't become a free-for-all because students aren't present. Instead, teachers use a ghost walk protocol to open up practice and gain insights from the environment about student learning.

Environmental aspects that teams focus on during ghost walks include how desks are arranged, how learning intentions and success criteria are posted, and how teachers use anchor charts, rubrics, and other tools to facilitate student learning. It is often useful to view firsthand how colleagues structure learning supports for students, as there's no one right way. While we may regularly visit a colleague's classroom to drop off a lesson plan or catch up about each other's weekends, typically we may not notice environmental learning supports unless there are specific cues, such as when expectations are predetermined and agreed upon before a ghost walk.

Ghost walks can be debriefed in similar ways as learning walks. Observational information is often presented as warm and cool feedback in the form of noticings and wonderings. Figure 5.5 offers a protocol your teams may consider using to debrief. When we enter another colleague's domain, we must be considerate of their feelings. It's much like being a guest at someone's house; we must be courteous so that we are invited back. That said, discussion-based protocols provide the rules, and emotional safety, for us to debrief authentically and honestly following a learning or ghost walk.

Information learned from vertical learning walks often assists teams to craft their next steps and ensure students are appropriately prepared for the next grade level.

Another type of ghost walk involves inviting family and community members to visit classrooms. These are scheduled so that families can sign up in advance. Teachers volunteer their classrooms and either the teacher, instructional coach, or principal facilitates discussions with the visitors. This is often enlightening for visitors as they gain a deeper understanding of where their children spend their days. Sometimes, visitors have mental models of classrooms based on their own experiences as students. Opening classroom doors and welcoming visitors in can help others update how they understand the school experience, as well as serve as opportunities to deepen connections between the home and school.

All observers, whether teachers, paraprofessionals, instructional coaches, administrators, or outside visitors, benefit from understanding the purpose and participating in the learning walk. As a reminder, it's important that all participants are made aware that these observations are not intended for spying on or evaluating teachers. They are neither punitive nor judgmental but instead are meant to offer glimpses into classroom life. Teams can use the questions in Figure 5.5 to prepare for their Learning Walks and Ghost Walks.

FIGURE 5.5   PREPARATION FOR LEARNING WALKS AND GHOST WALKS

1. **Establish the purpose for the walk.**

    Do observers need the purpose in writing?

2. **Discuss confidentiality.**

    What are the expectations about teachers' and students' privacy?

3. **Encourage learning.**

    If notes will be taken, how will this occur?

4. **Keep an open mind.**

    How will we respond if an inappropriate question is asked or judgment is made?

5. **Remember to observe, not evaluate.**

    Might an observational tool for outside visitors be helpful?

6. **Determine the time parameters.**

    How will the time be managed?

7. **Establish the ending point for the walk.**

    When will the learning walk be debriefed?

As with any observation, it works best when teams determine and agree upon the observation tool in advance of the learning walk or ghost walk. Teams might also consider labeling the observations by classroom, which also provides a degree of anonymity to teachers being observed. In this way, teams are better positioned to focus on evidence, rather than on the teacher. Teams are encouraged to use the observation tool shown in Figure 5.6 to assist with this process.

FIGURE 5.6   LEARNING WALK AND GHOST WALK OBSERVATION TOOL

	EVIDENCE	NOTES	WONDERINGS
Classroom A			
Classroom B			
Classroom C			

DEBRIEFING LEARNING WALKS AND GHOST WALKS

After a learning walk or ghost walk, teams debrief in structured ways to avoid evaluative language that may be hurtful and shut down the process. A facilitator can lead the process by providing reminders to observers and prompting for individual reflection before team members share aloud. This assists team members to articulate factual observations based upon the evidence, their notes, and wonderings related to the evidence-based practice. Facilitators and teams can refer to the guide in Figure 5.7 to formulate evidence-based statements for the team to discuss when debriefing.

FIGURE 5.7 FACILITATOR GUIDE FOR DEBRIEFING LEARNING AND GHOST WALKS

REMINDERS FOR DEBRIEFING	MY THOUGHTS	OUR COLLECTIVE THOUGHTS
Evidence This isn't an observation of the teacher. What is the specific evidence seen? Try not to speculate.		
Evaluative Language Try to avoid using "I liked . . ." or "I didn't like . . ." Describe what you saw, not how you feel about it.		
Evidence-Based Practice Were any commonalities noticed across classrooms? Are any patterns beginning to emerge?		

MICROTEACHING

Another way teachers open up practice is through microteaching. Microteaching is an observation of a recorded lesson. No fancy equipment or setup is needed; just your phone or a tablet will do. As with other learning walks, there are certain protocols that can be used to focus the observation of the microteaching. Usually, the length of the video doesn't exceed 10 minutes and the host teacher can start and stop the video at the appropriate markers to get feedback from a peer coach. For example, the teacher being observed asks a colleague for feedback based upon the questions she asked during guided instruction. That becomes the section of the video that is viewed together at a later time.

There are many benefits to using the microteaching strategy. It's free, fast, and there isn't a need for substitutes because the teachers can determine a time to meet that's convenient for both of them. Microteaching can take place during a prep period, at lunch, before or after school, or even from home, since the video can be viewed by both teachers. Another benefit of microteaching is that the teacher being observed can preview the video before meeting with the peer coach. Since the teacher being observed controls when the video starts and stops, this is an additional layer of emotional safety. During this debrief, the peer coach uses their Cognitive Coaching skills to assist the teacher being observed to unpack their thinking about the lesson.

◄ DOUG EXPLAINS THE BENEFITS OF MICROTEACHING
resources.corwin.com/collectiveefficacy

Like other classroom observations, microteaching is non-evaluative, so teachers use terms like *noticings* and *wonderings* during their discussions. Since many educators are hesitant to be recorded (lest the "evidence" be used against them by an evaluator), many schools who use the microteaching strategy have an established procedure to delete the video file following the discussion. By deleting the video file, the teacher is protected, and students' confidentiality is maintained. If team members adhere to the protocol, using the video only for instructional purposes, there isn't a need to obtain parental consent for students to appear in a video.

Just as face-to-face classroom observations are scheduled, teachers do the same thing using the microteaching strategy. After the first round of observation, reflection, and discussion, the pair then reverses roles. Now there is a different host teacher who provides the focus of the lesson observation. Microteaching works really well during a Collective Efficacy Cycle because teachers can watch the video multiple times, and in doing so have multiple exposures to the evidence-based practice.

Discussion-based protocols provide the rules, and emotional safety, for us to debrief authentically and honestly.

FORMAL COACHING

Kraft and colleagues (2017) examined sixty studies about instructional coaching to determine the effect on student achievement by strengthening teachers' practice. From this meta-analysis, which is a synthesis of many studies, the researchers found that coaching improves the quality of an educator's practice *by as much as a decade of experience* in teaching. This suggests that coaching has a much stronger effect than traditional professional development methods.

Further, it was learned that larger coaching initiatives are less effective than smaller initiatives. The quality of coaching was likely decreased during large initiatives because more skilled coaches were needed. There is also the possibility that a large initiative may have standardized the coaching objectives, rather than individualizing for each teacher. This meta-analysis revealed that individualized guidance is critical to the success of coaching.

Opening classroom doors and welcoming visitors in can help others update how they understand the school experience.

COGNITIVE COACHING

During Collective Efficacy Cycles, teachers often gain skills in Cognitive Coaching as they collaborate, reflect, and debrief with their colleagues. Cognitive Coaching differs from other types of coaching in that it's a process in which teachers explore the thinking behind their practices. One way to think about your thinking is by considering your mind as an unfinished map. During Cognitive Coaching, questions are asked by the coach to reveal areas of the map that aren't complete yet (Garmston et al., 1993). As teachers process out loud, the reasons why they made particular decisions become clearer, thus adding to their maps. Cognitive Coaching, then, is a guided reflection that enhances teachers' intellectual growth by improving one's ability to self-monitor, self-analyze, and self-evaluate.

During the early cycles of Cognitive Coaching, the coach facilitates the teacher's ability to complete their cognitive map. In essence, with Cognitive Coaching experience, people are often able to add details to their cognitive maps on their own. This heightened awareness of thinking causes people to look beyond their gut instincts and consider the actual reasons why they made those decisions.

◀ NANCY DESCRIBES HOW
COGNITIVE COACHING WORKS
resources.corwin.com/collectiveefficacy

NOTES

_____

_____

_____

_____

_____

_____

_____

_____

_____

_____

_____

_____

ACT 2: WORK SMARTER, NOT HARDER

Kara, a new tenth-grade biology teacher at Hyatt High, participates in a Cognitive Coaching cycle with other members of the science department during a recent Collective Efficacy Cycle. The focus is on encouraging students to participate in classroom discussions during a unit about interdependent relationships in ecosystems. Kara, being new to teaching and her team, is concerned that her colleagues might think less of her if they observe her instruction. She is also nervous about participating in Cognitive Coaching since she doesn't know what it's all about. During team meetings, when the science teachers discuss strategies to enhance students' participation in classroom discussions, Kara chimes in because she feels confident about her content knowledge.

The science teachers adhere to the eight-week schedule they had co-developed for the Collective Efficacy Cycle. Kara knows that the period of Safe Practice is quickly coming to an end and that the expectation for peer observations is approaching. She isn't quite sure how it is all going to go down until the meeting when the teachers determine their peer observation schedule. Joy, one of the more experienced teachers, says to the team, "We've been doing this [Cognitive Coaching] for a couple of years now, but this is Kara's first rodeo. Kara, how about if you double up with me so you can see how this works? If you're okay with it, I'd like you to be an extra observer when Jason coaches me. You can be there for the pre-observation, and you can go with him to the observation, and we can debrief for the post-conference in my classroom after school next Tuesday. Does that work for you?" Kara is relieved and feels off the hook for now. She is more intrigued to see how Cognitive Coaching would work with one of her mentors. Kara wonders if Joy would be nervous with two additional teachers in her classroom while she was practicing wait time with students.

The following Tuesday morning, Joy, Jason, and Kara meet for the pre-observation conference. During this initial meeting, Jason asks Joy just four questions while Kara observes. The questions Jason asks are

1. What are your learning intentions?
2. How will you know when you've reached your objectives?
3. How will students know they've been successful?
4. What aspects of your teaching would you like information about from me?

Coaching improves the quality of an educator's practice *by as much as a decade of experience* in teaching.

Joy considers each question, responding thoughtfully. Both Jason and Kara take notes to ensure they can provide Joy with the information she requested when they meet again during the post-conference. Kara is pleasantly surprised that this initial meeting lasts only about 15 minutes. Later that day, Jason and Kara arrive at Joy's classroom at the agreed-upon time for the observation. Since Joy had requested that they gather information about student-student interactions, both Jason and Kara took notes. For the second time that day, Kara is surprised by the process and how non-threatening it is. Joy is very comfortable having others in her classroom;

she said she was used to it and welcomes feedback from her colleagues. Kara feels much better about having her colleagues observe her.

The following morning, the three teachers reconvene for the post-observation conference. Kara isn't quite sure how Jason is going to handle this conversation, because she had noticed several students who didn't participate in the conversations about interdependence in ecosystems. She wonders how Jason will approach this since student participation in these conversations is the whole goal for the lesson and Collective Efficacy Cycle. Jason, skilled in Cognitive Coaching, begins the debrief by asking Joy how she thought the lesson went and if anything went differently than she had planned. Kara watches Joy think through her lesson intentions and what transpired in the classroom. Kay notices that Jason doesn't talk much during the post-conference. Instead, Joy does most of the talking, reflecting upon the instructional decisions she made and the impact on student learning.

Part of being a skilled Cognitive Coach is knowing when silence will elicit a response and when verbal prompting is needed.

To Kara's surprise, the post-conference is also fairly quick and painless. She worries that Joy might become defensive if she or Jason bring up their observations about how some students were not participating, but they don't need to raise this point because Joy is already aware of it—she brings it up herself. As she reflects aloud, Joy considers her own actions that contributed to students not participating. Joy doesn't blame students, call them apathetic, or make excuses for students not participating. Instead, Joy takes responsibility because she realizes that she wasn't providing enough space for students to process and converse. By processing out loud, Joy recognizes how she could improve her own teaching. Neither Jason nor Kara has to tell her because she realizes it for herself.

It doesn't always happen this easily. At times, the Cognitive Coach may have to do a bit more prompting to foster deeper reflection. Part of being a skilled Cognitive Coach is knowing when silence will elicit a response and when verbal prompting is needed.

Kara and her science department colleagues became better thinkers, and thus better teachers, because of their experience with Cognitive Coaching. Over time, Kara realized she was also becoming more bicognitive. Being bicognitive is the ability to simultaneously attend to "both relationship and task, to be both student- *and* teacher-centered" (Garmston et al., 1993, p. 60). Guided reflection helped Kara to enhance her problem-solving skills while she developed her instructional repertoire. Examining her practice, generating alternatives in the moment, and self-assessing became standard practices for Kara. Her comfort was increased because her growth was supported through experimentation and continued collaboration with her colleagues. The other science teachers modeled taking risks, being open minded, and striving for continual improvement. The culture of adult learning continues to be strong at Hyatt High, and because they esteem metacognition, Kara and her colleagues now use these same coaching prompts with their students.

MODULE 5 RECAP: WHAT DID WE LEARN?

Yay, team! Opening up practice for peer observations promotes collaboration, support, and teamwork among teachers and creates a culture where we all share a strong sense of community and collective responsibility for our student's success. It's job-embedded professional learning, and no one is pulled out to attend a workshop or travel to a conference. Instead, peer observations are structured opportunities to learn with and from each other. Questions to consider at the end of the Opening Up Practice phase include

- Did each team member participate and adhere to the pre-conference, observation, post-conference structure?
- Was feedback provided in the form of neutral descriptions of facts observed in the classroom?
- In what ways is reflection prompting the team's professional knowledge?

Peer observations are structured opportunities to learn with and from each other.

NOTES

_____

_____

_____

_____

_____

_____

_____

_____

_____

_____

_____

_____

_____

_____

_____

_____

_____

_____

_____

FIGURE 5.8 COLLECTIVE EFFICACY CYCLE REFLECTIVE QUESTIONS

QUESTION	MY THOUGHTS/DEGREE OF COLLECTIVE EFFICACY				
Mastery Experiences: In what ways was our team successful? Identify specific instances when our actions were skillful.	1	2	3	4	5
Trust: Was there a sense of trust among the team while determining the common challenge? Note instances when trust was strong.	1	2	3	4	5
Problem Solving: In what ways did we work together to solve problems? Describe when and how the team supported each other.	1	2	3	4	5
Assets-Orientation: When faced with a problem, did we maintain an assets-oriented stance? Note any situations when the team built upon students' strengths, interests, and background knowledge.	1	2	3	4	5
Efficiency: Did we adhere to agreed-upon protocols and use our time well? Write down times when our meetings felt productive.	1	2	3	4	5
Optimism: What was the general tenor/emotional tone of our meetings? Describe instances when we supported each other to maintain a positive outlook.	1	2	3	4	5

Access videos and resources for this module at
resources.corwin.com/collectiveefficacy

Module 6
MONITORING, MODIFYING, AND CELEBRATING

MODULE OVERVIEW

Once your team has engaged in peer observations and learning walks, the Collective Efficacy Cycle comes to a close. We have worked hard to learn an evidence-based strategy, strengthen our knowledge and skills, and increase student learning. In addition to formative assessment, we also gathered information from students about their learning experiences during the cycle. Using all the data, let's share ideas about what worked well and what could be improved next time. Importantly, celebrating student learning and team successes is vital to generating collective teacher efficacy. It is during the closure phase that we self-assess and determine if participating in the cycle created a mastery experience. Additionally, closure provides opportunities to invite other educators to view artifacts and provide feedback from the Collective Efficacy Cycle process through a gallery walk.

◀ INTRODUCTION TO MODULE 6
resources.corwin.com/collectiveefficacy

A gallery walk allows teams to design a visual representation of their learning and student progress over the past six to eight weeks. This process supports reflection and offers a mechanism for other educators and teams to view the learning progression at a time that's convenient for them. A visual representation provides the means for others to learn from this team through a vicarious experience. The Innovation Configuration Map displayed in Figure 6.1 provides a description of what ideal closure looks like as this Collective Efficacy Cycle comes to an end.

◀ EMPOWERING TEACHERS BY CELEBRATING EFFORTS
resources.corwin.com/collectiveefficacy

FIGURE 6.1 INNOVATION CONFIGURATION (IC) MAP FOR MONITORING, MODIFYING, AND CELEBRATING

1: IDEAL STATE	2: DEVELOPING	3: STARTING OUT
The Collective Efficacy Cycle comes to a close by meeting **all** of the following criteria.	The Collective Efficacy Cycle comes to a close by meeting **most** (50–99%) of the success criteria.	The Collective Efficacy Cycle comes to a close by meeting **some** (0–49%) of the success criteria.

Team members

- Gather information from students about their learning experience

- Evaluate the impact of the evidence-based practice by analyzing multiple sources of data

- Determine if the cycle was a mastery experience

- Identify future areas for professional learning

- Plan a gallery walk using artifacts from the cycle and invite colleagues to view, ask questions, and comment

EDUCATORS' INDEPENDENT REFLECTIONS

Just as teachers encourage students to accept critique and revise their work, teams also engage in introspection to identify successes and next steps. It's important that teams set aside time for this last component of the Collective Efficacy Cycle. Through analysis, teams determine if the cycle resulted in a mastery experience. This occurs through independent (Figure 6.2) and team reflections (Figure 6.3), as well as through analysis of student learning. Teams gather formative assessment data, artifacts that demonstrate student work and learning, and survey information from students about their learning experiences throughout the cycle.

◄ **THE TEAM DISCUSSES THEIR SENSE OF MASTERY**
resources.corwin.com/collectiveefficacy

NOTES

_____
_____
_____
_____
_____
_____
_____

FIGURE 6.2 INDEPENDENT REFLECTION

INDEPENDENT REFLECTION QUESTIONS	MY THOUGHTS
1. What learning needs did the study of the selected evidence-based practice meet? What further professional learning could I pursue?	
2. How has my teaching practice been validated or changed as a result of this learning?	
3. How has this cycle impacted student outcomes? What evidence informs this?	
4. How can I share my learning experience with other colleagues outside of the team?	

FIGURE 6.3 SUCCESS ANALYSIS PROTOCOL

Purpose: Using student learning information and teacher experience, teams analyze the implementation of the evidence-based practice.

STEPS	NOTES
1. **Identify Success(es)** Each team member reflects and writes a short description of one or more successful aspects of the Collective Efficacy Cycle.	
2. **Share Successes** In rounds, each team member shares aloud until all ideas have been heard.	
3. **Clarifying Questions** Clarifying questions are posed and answered.	
4. **Independent Reflection of Top Three Successes** Each team member decides their top three successes of all ideas shared.	
5. **Consensus on Top Three Successes** Teams discuss and collaboratively determine the top three successes that are shared by the team.	
6. **Celebrate!**	

STUDENT SURVEYS AND INTERVIEWS

Student surveys and interviews provide useful feedback about their experience with the evidence-based practice. Even young children can respond to a small number of questions orally and through the use of pictures. Older students are often able to provide insights related to learning that may not have occurred to us.

◄ STRATEGIES TO SHARE COLLECTIVE KNOWLEDGE
resources.corwin.com/collectiveefficacy

GALLERY WALKS

A gallery walk provides opportunities for all stakeholders to see work being done throughout the school and to ask questions about the process. They see differences in approaches, progressions, gaps in the progressions, and next steps. A gallery walk helps people to become more familiar with educators' plans and students' experiences; see Figure 6.4 for a facilitation guide.

◄ A SIXTH GRADER'S PERSPECTIVE ABOUT HIS LEARNING EXPERIENCE
resources.corwin.com/collectiveefficacy

NOTES

_____
_____
_____
_____
_____
_____
_____
_____
_____
_____
_____
_____
_____
_____
_____
_____
_____
_____

FIGURE 6.4 GALLERY WALK FACILITATION GUIDE

	NOTES
Encourage Written Feedback Determine how and when feedback is collected: • Pens • Sticky notes • Handouts • QR codes • T-charts	
Observations, Not Evaluations Ensure people are primed to provide observational feedback, not judgments. Ask that viewers • Remain curious • Ask questions that begin with "I'm wondering about . . ." and "I'm wondering if . . ."	
Knowledge Sharing Prepare for any handouts: • Evidence-based practice • Professional reading suggestions • Visual schedule • Links to videos	
Permissions Clarify whether audience members have permission to take, view, or post photos and/or videos: • Photographs • Social media • School blog or other sites	
Reflective Questions for Audience Members • *In what ways does this impact your own practice?* • *What do you want to learn more about?*	

WHAT A CULTURE OF COLLECTIVE EFFICACY SOUNDS LIKE

When there is a culture of collective efficacy, student learning is emphasized and there is a genuine belief that educators in this school are equipped to ensure positive student outcomes. Educators who take collective responsibility and internal accountability are the norm. Discussions of instructional practices are grounded by evidence of student learning, and asset-oriented language is used to describe student needs. Figure 6.5 offers insights into how a school environment sounds when collective efficacy is present.

FIGURE 6.5   WHAT A CULTURE OF COLLECTIVE EFFICACY SOUNDS LIKE

COLLECTIVE EFFICACY SOUNDS LIKE . . .	COLLECTIVE EFFICACY DOESN'T SOUND LIKE . . .
• "The way we talk about learning sets the tone for our students in terms of what they think is possible for them to achieve. If we want students to rise to meet challenges, we need to normalize errors and mistakes as opportunities to learn."	• "Nothing we do will make any difference. The kids don't care and their parents don't value education."
• "What learning experiences can we design together to make sure our students are working at an appropriate level of challenge in biology?"	• "There's not a lot we can do to improve our kids' reading skills when they don't read at home."
• "The teachers in the third-grade PLC implemented this reading strategy in their classrooms and their students are getting really good results. Let's check out what's happening in their classrooms so that we can consider how we might better support our students' reading abilities."	• "When they learn to follow instructions, we can begin working on their reading and writing."
	• "They just don't get it."
• "By working together, our students achieve so much more."	• "It is not their fault. They've had to deal with so much trauma."

SCALING SUCCESS

The Collective Efficacy Cycle is a means for us to be inspired in the present and to take action to achieve our aspirations. Scaling this from a team level to a school level requires organizational readiness. The questions in Figure 6.6 and Figure 6.7 can assist teams and school administrators in determining areas of strength and next steps.

FIGURE 6.6 TOOL TO ASSESS ORGANIZATIONAL READINESS TO SCALE

QUESTIONS	MY THOUGHTS	OUR COLLECTIVE THOUGHTS
Self-Worth		
1. In what ways do school administrators provide team-building opportunities for educators?		
2. Are educators' accomplishments frequently celebrated in the school? In what ways?		
3. How do leaders know the hopes and dreams of teachers?		
Engagement		
4. In what ways do school administrators encourage educators to be creative?		
5. How does the school environment encourage educators to have fun?		
6. In what ways do educators have input into professional learning offerings?		
7. In what ways do principals and other leaders encourage educators to take healthy risks and let them know they are supported, whether they are successful or not?		
Purpose		
8. In what ways are educators encouraged to set their own professional goals?		
9. What types of authentic opportunities do educators have to assume leadership roles that align with their interests and strengths?		

Source: Adapted from Quaglia and Lande (2017).

FIGURE 6.7 COLLECTIVE EFFICACY CYCLE REFLECTIVE QUESTIONS

QUESTION	MY THOUGHTS/DEGREE OF COLLECTIVE EFFICACY				
Mastery Experiences: In what ways was our team successful? Identify specific instances when our actions were skillful.	1	2	3	4	5
Trust: Was there a sense of trust among the team while determining the common challenge? Note instances when trust was strong.	1	2	3	4	5
Problem Solving: In what ways did we work together to solve problems? Describe when and how the team supported each other.	1	2	3	4	5
Assets-Orientation: When faced with a problem, did we maintain an assets-oriented stance? Note any situations when the team built upon students' strengths, interests, and background knowledge.	1	2	3	4	5
Efficiency: Did we adhere to agreed-upon protocols and use our time well? Write down times when our meetings felt productive.	1	2	3	4	5
Optimism: What was the general tenor/emotional tone of our meetings? Describe instances when we supported each other to maintain a positive outlook.	1	2	3	4	5

MODULE 6 RECAP: WHAT DID WE LEARN?

Yay, team! We did it!

Using student learning assessment, information from student surveys, and structured reflections, we monitored and adjusted the evidence-based practice so that our students are successful. At the close of the cycle, we shared ideas about what worked well and what could be improved next time. Celebrating student learning and team successes is essential for teams to generate collective teacher efficacy. Additionally, a gallery walk created the opportunity for other educators to view artifacts and provide feedback directly from the Collective Efficacy Cycle process.

When the gallery walk concludes, it's important we make a final self-assessment. Let's consider the feedback provided by other educators and stakeholders during the gallery walk and reflect using the questions in Figure 6.8. When a Collective Efficacy Cycle culminates, we encourage administrators, coaches, and district leaders to both commend and affirm the efforts of educators.

◀ CLOSING THOUGHTS
resources.corwin.com/collectiveefficacy

NOTES

_____

_____

_____

_____

_____

_____

_____

_____

_____

_____

_____

_____

_____

_____

_____

_____

_____

_____

_____

FIGURE 6.8   INDIVIDUAL AND TEAM ASSESSMENT OF THE COLLECTIVE EFFICACY CYCLE

	MY THOUGHTS	OUR COLLECTIVE THOUGHTS
Self-Efficacy		
1. In what ways has my confidence grown?		
2. How has my knowledge grown throughout this cycle?		
3. Did I meet my own expectations for success?		
Collective Efficacy		
4. Did our team execute the plans we created?		
5. In what ways did our collective knowledge strengthen?		
6. Was our collective goal attained?		
7. Was our collective goal challenging enough?		
8. In what ways has the team grown closer?		
9. Did our collective efforts result in a mastery experience?		

Describe:

Did our collective efforts initiate a vicarious experience for other educators?

What actions will we continue to take as a team?

Where do we need to improve?

What are some early ideas for the next Collective Efficacy Cycle?

Access videos and resources for this module at
resources.corwin.com/collectiveefficacy

CONCLUSION

Educators face many challenges—it seems that requirements and expectations change frequently, and new programs arrive every year with the promise of "fixing" a problem at the school. This heavy load can feel overwhelming when we face these challenges alone. Instead, we can decrease levels of stress by collaborating with other educators in ways that cultivate collective teacher efficacy. Collective teacher efficacy both causes and results from increased student achievement.

Teaching and learning matter.

> High skills × high challenge + success = collective teacher efficacy

Rather than lamenting challenges, effective teams are positioned to identify student needs, collectively generate solutions, and implement them. Educators and administrators can share ownership of the teaching and learning environment and ensure everyone's well-being. In the ideal situation, your team nurtures and sustains collective teacher efficacy such that it becomes the norm—it's how the school operates. Once collective teacher efficacy becomes the fabric of a system, it's difficult to imagine going back to a traditional school environment where classroom doors are closed and each teacher is a lone wolf. Collectively, we can create cultures that cultivate collective teacher efficacy and allow it to thrive.

> Three Specific, Fundamental Actions That Generate Collective Teacher Efficacy
>
> 1. Implementing evidence-based practices with students
> 2. Determining and attaining a shared goal
> 3. Opening up practice through peer observations

Teaching and learning matter. Finding purpose, mastery, and mindfulness within the company of our colleagues can mitigate some, or many, of the stressors educators feel while at school. Through deep connections with team members, we can cultivate peak moments and generate collective flow while serving our students, families, and communities. Educators appreciate coffee gift cards and mugs full of chocolate candies, but our biggest joy comes from knowing our work makes the world just a little bit better.

APPENDICES

RESOURCES FOR TEAMS

The tools included in the appendices have been supplied for those teams who wish to examine or deepen other aspects of their collaboration.

A. Collective Efficacy Cycle Visual Schedule Template

B. Innovation Configuration (IC) Map Action Planner

C. Trust on Our Team

D. Self-Assessment for Individual Contributions to Meetings

E. Successful Meetings Card Sort Activity

F. Benefits of Recording Notes Visibly and Publicly

G. Tips for Productive PLC+ Meetings

H. Conflict in Teams

I. Facilitating Consensus

J. Focusing Four Consensus Protocol

K. Group Dynamics in PLC+ Meetings

Access videos and resources for the appendices at
resources.corwin.com/collectiveefficacy

A. COLLECTIVE EFFICACY CYCLE VISUAL SCHEDULE TEMPLATE

Common Challenge:

Evidence-Based Strategy:

CYCLE # DATE SPAN:	COMMON CHALLENGE Dialogue about student learning needs	BUILDING KNOWLEDGE Professional learning for staff to implement an evidence-based practice	SAFE PRACTICE Educators experiment with the new practice in a low-risk environment	PROFESSIONAL READING Teachers receive professional articles relevant to the practice being learned	OPENING UP PRACTICE Educators observe each other and engage in structured reflections and feedback	MONITORING, MODIFYING, AND CELEBRATING Educators engage in learning walks during and after school to discuss student learning	NEXT STEPS Teachers review evidence of student learning and determine next steps
Week 1:							
Week 2:							
Week 3:							
Week 4:							

| CYCLE # | COMMON CHALLENGE | BUILDING KNOWLEDGE | SAFE PRACTICE | PROFESSIONAL READING | OPENING UP PRACTICE | MONITORING, MODIFYING, AND CELEBRATING | NEXT STEPS |
DATE SPAN:	Dialogue about student learning needs	Professional learning for staff to implement an evidence-based practice	Educators experiment with the new practice in a low-risk environment	Teachers receive professional articles relevant to the practice being learned	Educators observe each other and engage in structured reflections and feedback	Educators engage in learning walks during and after school to discuss student learning	Teachers review evidence of student learning and determine next steps
Week 5:							
Week 6:							
Week 7:							
Week 8:							

B. INNOVATION CONFIGURATION (IC) MAP ACTION PLANNER

An Innovation Configuration (IC) Map provides teams with an understanding of what ideal implementation of each component of the Collective Efficacy Cycle looks like. As you take steps toward these optimal conditions, teams might find it helpful to use this IC Map Action Planner to reflect on strengths and next steps in relation to the PLC+ framework.

Collective Efficacy Cycle _____

PLC+ Framework Guiding Questions

1. **Where are we going?**

2. **Where are we now?**

3. **How do we move learning forward?**

4. **What did we learn today?**

5. **Who benefited and who did not benefit?**

	STRENGTHS	NEXT STEPS
Module 1: Developing Individual and Collective Efficacy		
Module 2: Determining the Common Challenge		
Module 3: Building Educator Knowledge and Skills		
Module 4: Collaborative Planning and Safe Practice		
Module 5: Collaborative Planning and Opening Up Practice		
Module 6: Monitoring, Modifying, and Celebrating		

C. TRUST ON OUR TEAM

The importance of a positive school culture can't be overemphasized. It's the key to high-performing teams, an effective learning environment, and a stronger school community. Without it, even the best plans will fall short.

	MY THOUGHTS	OUR COLLECTIVE THOUGHTS
Mutual Respect: How the team operates and communicates		
Personal Regard: An individual's openness and sharing of personal information		
Competence in Core Responsibilities: Each team member has specific responsibilities, and all are dependent on each other to enact a course of action		
Personal Integrity: One's honesty and reliability		

D. SELF-ASSESSMENT FOR INDIVIDUAL CONTRIBUTIONS TO MEETINGS

Use the following tool for personal reflection and goal setting.

CRITERIA	HOW CONSISTENT AM I?	WHAT IS THE SPECIFIC GOAL FOR OUR NEXT MEETING?
I strive to make contributions to each meeting by sharing reflections about instructional practices openly.		
I use evidence of student learning, including work products, assessments, or other artifacts when discussing instruction.		
I raise questions in thoughtful ways that push the group's thinking and deepen our collective understanding.		
I paraphrase what others say to communicate that I am listening carefully.		
I am mindful of not talking too much because others also have contributions to make.		

E. SUCCESSFUL MEETINGS CARD SORT ACTIVITY

Open-Ended Version

Purpose: To foster collective efficacy through social cohesion. Individuals share beliefs and experiences related to professional learning that have been impactful. Team members gain a deeper understanding of how to structure collaborative processes that meet the needs of all team members. By considering these elements, the team increases its own clarity about collaborative work.

Materials Needed: 3 × 5 index cards

Suggested Time: 30 minutes

Facilitator Notes: This activity can be done in groups or with a whole staff. If working with a staff, determine how groups will be established prior to beginning the activity.

Step 1: Individual reflection (3 minutes)

Individuals independently generate concrete examples of experiences, strategies, and tools seen or used in successful meetings. Each idea is recorded on a 3 × 5 card. Write one idea per card legibly so others can read them. Names are optional.

Step 2: Sharing in home groups (12 minutes)

Each person shares and explains one or more of their index cards. Groups arrange cards into categories and determine labels for each. Prepare for a gallery walk by ensuring cards and labels are understandable to other groups.

Step 3: Gallery walk (5 minutes)

Groups move about the room to read others' displays. Take note of additional compelling ideas.

Step 4: Return to home groups (5 minutes)

Discuss ideas and connections made during the gallery walk. Participants can add thoughts to the group's collection. Identify ideas that are unnecessary or lower priority and remove these cards.

Step 5: Consolidate ideas (5 minutes)

Collaboratively determine the group's top three to five ideas for successful meetings and discuss how these ideas might be enacted.

Focused-Responses Version

Purpose: To foster collective efficacy through social cohesion. Individuals share impactful professional learning experiences, core values, optimal learning conditions, and three wishes for the school. By focusing on these elements, teams increase their own clarity about collaborative work.

Materials Needed: 3 × 5 index cards

Suggested Time: 30 minutes

Facilitator Notes: This activity can be done in groups or with a whole staff. If working with a staff, determine how groups will be established prior to beginning the activity.

Step 1: Individual reflection (3 minutes)

Individuals independently respond to the prompts on the next page. Each idea is recorded on a 3 × 5 card. Write one idea per card legibly so others can read them. Names are optional.

Step 2: Sharing in home groups (12 minutes)

Each person shares and explains one or more of their index cards. Groups arrange cards into categories and determine labels for each. Prepare for a gallery walk by ensuring cards and labels are understandable to other groups.

Step 3: Gallery walk (5 minutes)

Groups move about the room to read others' displays. Take note of additional compelling ideas.

Step 4: Return to home groups (5 minutes)

Discuss ideas and connections made during the gallery walk. Participants can add thoughts to the group's collection. Identify ideas that are unnecessary or lower priority and remove these cards.

Step 5: Consolidate ideas (5 minutes)

Collaboratively determine the group's top three to five ideas for successful meetings and discuss how these ideas might be enacted.

BEST EXPERIENCES	CORE VALUES	OPTIMAL CONDITIONS	THREE WISHES
Describe your best professional learning experience. When did you feel most alive and engaged? What made it so exciting? Who was there? Describe the experience in detail.	Explain what you value most deeply—things about yourself, your relationships, and your work.	What are the key ingredients, both internal and external, that enable you to be at your best and to find enjoyment and satisfaction in your work?	If you were granted three wishes for this school and students, what would they be?

F. BENEFITS OF RECORDING NOTES VISIBLY AND PUBLICLY

- Helps the group focus on the task at hand

- Depersonalizes ideas and data

- Enhances participants' memories during and after a meeting

- Frees participants from taking notes

- Develops shared ownership

- Discourages repetition and circular conversations

- Encourages participation by providing equal weight to individuals' ideas

- Enables each member to check and make sure their ideas are being recorded accurately

- Increases the group's sense of accomplishment

- Promotes more sophisticated problem-solving methods by holding onto information developed in one sitting for use in the next

- Makes it easier for latecomers to catch up without interrupting the meeting

- Ensures accountability; decisions, responsibilities, and dates are written down

G. TIPS FOR PRODUCTIVE PLC+ MEETINGS

BEFORE	NOTES
• Co-develop an agenda with a detailed purpose, outcomes, and time allocations. • Distribute the agenda to each person. • Gather materials (chart paper, markers, electronic document, etc.). • Establish roles. • Review shared agreements.	

DURING	NOTES
• Discussions and/or activities should match agenda items. • When time is up for an agenda item, decide whether to stop or continue. • Have a "parking lot" chart for ideas to revisit.	

CLOSURE	NOTES
• Check in about process. • Determine next steps and next meeting date. • Share notes with team.	

H. CONFLICT IN TEAMS

Conflict in teams is natural; it's neither positive nor negative. It just is. Conflict can improve team effectiveness. The key is to maintain *cognitive* conflict, rather than *affective* conflict.

COGNITIVE CONFLICT	AFFECTIVE CONFLICT
Disagreements about fundamental differences of opinion can enhance team effectiveness by eliciting	Disagreements over individualized personally oriented matters diminish team effectiveness and lead to
• Improved decisions	• Destructive conflict
• Raised commitment levels	• Less effective decisions
• Stronger cohesiveness	• Diminished commitment
• Enhanced empathy	• Reduced cohesiveness
• Deeper understanding	• Limited empathy

Source: Adapted from Garmston and Wellman (1999).

Teams that use cognitive conflict without producing affective conflict develop capabilities that other teams do not have. PLCs that encourage cognitive conflict are:

- **More focused.** They are less likely to allow distractions to interrupt their momentum.

- **More creative.** These teams encourage expanded thinking and listen to voices that may have been marginalized in the past. They are inclusive of different perspectives and apply new approaches to problems of practice.

- **More expressive.** They maintain open communication and challenge each other's assumptions. They seek out opinions and democratize each person's contributions.

- **More inclusive.** They have a culture that encourages equity—your voice without the threat of anger, animosity, or punishment.

Note times when cognitive conflict promotes team learning. When is a team learning challenged?

CURRENT APPROACHES TO TEAM LEARNING	IDEAS TO STRENGTHEN

I. FACILITATING CONSENSUS

Facilitating consensus means that all participants have a voice in the decision-making process. Differences of opinion are viewed as helpful rather than an impediment. Each person is given a chance to describe their feelings about the issue and those who continue to disagree indicate publicly that they are willing to go along for an experimental try for a prescribed amount of time. Everyone shares in the final decision.

Suggestions for effective consensus decision making:

- Avoid arguing for your own position.
- When at an impasse, avoid feelings of winning and losing by determining the most acceptable option for everyone.
- Don't change your mind just to avoid conflict.
- Avoid conflict-reducing methods such as majority vote, averages, coin toss, and bargaining.

Facilitating consensus does not mean:

- A unanimous vote
- Everyone's first choice
- That everyone agrees

J. FOCUSING FOUR CONSENSUS PROTOCOL

Facilitator notes:

- Explain the process and facilitator's role before beginning the activity.
- Clarify any questions.
- Explain that advocacy at the survey stage will not make the decision. The group will decide and be guided, not bound, by the data.

1. **Brainstorm**	• The group individually brainstorms ideas. • The group shares and records ideas on a chart, discouraging criticisms or questions and aiming for eight to 10 ideas.
2. **Clarify**	• The facilitator asks if any items need to be clarified. • The author of the idea provides clarification. • The facilitator stops the clarification when the person asking the question indicates nonverbally or otherwise that they understand.
3. **Advocate**	• Participants may advocate for as many items as they wish and as many times as they wish. • Advocacy statements must be phrased positively. • Advocacy statements must be brief.
4. **Survey**	• The group individually reflects about which ideas they feel are most important. • The facilitator takes a hand count to determine the ideas most important to the group. • The group collaboratively identifies and agrees upon the best option.

Source: Adapted from Garmston and Wellman (1999).

K. GROUP DYNAMICS IN PLC+ MEETINGS

	REFLECTIONS	THOUGHTS FOR IMPROVEMENT
Flight: A person's tendency to avoid or flee from a problem		
Fight: An individual trying to convince or cajole others		
Pairing: Side conversations and/or alliances that interfere with a group's maturation		
Dependency: The person depending on others to carry their load		

Source: Adapted from Garmston and Wellman (1999).

REFERENCES

Bandura, A. (1977). Self-efficacy: Toward a unifying theory of behavioral change. *Psychological Review, 84*(2), 191–215.

Bandura, A. (1997). *Self-efficacy: The exercise of control*. Freeman.

Bandura, A. (2000). Exercise of human agency through collective efficacy. *Current Directions in Psychological Science, 9*(3), 75–78.

Bird, T., & Little, J. W. (1986). How schools organize the teaching occupation. *Elementary School Journal, 86*(4), 493–511.

Blanchard, K. (2009). *Feedback is the breakfast of champions*. https://www.kenblanchardbooks .com/feedback-is-the-breakfast-of-champions

Calvert, L. (2016). *Moving from compliance to agency: What teachers need to make professional learning work*. Learning Forward and National Commission on Teaching and America's Future.

Cialdini, R. B. (2007). *Influence: The psychology of persuasion*. Collins.

City, E. A., Elmore, R. F., Fiarman, S. E., & Teitel, L. (2010). *Instructional rounds in education: A network approach to improving learning and teaching*. Harvard Education Press.

Csikszentmihalyi, M. (1990). *Flow: The psychology of optimal experience*. Harper and Row.

Czach, C. (2020). How to practice reframing during stressful situations at work. *Forbes*.

Darling-Hammond, L., Hyler, M. E., & Gardner, M. (2017). *Effective teacher professional development*. Learning Policy Institute.

Deans for Impact. (2016). *Practice with purpose: The emerging science of teacher expertise*. Author.

Ericsson, A., & Pool, R. (2016). *Peak: Secrets from the new science of expertise*. Houghton Mifflin Harcourt.

Evans, A. (2009). No Child Left Behind and the quest for educational equity: The role of teachers' collective sense of efficacy. *Leadership and Policy in Schools, 8*, 64–91.

Evans, M., Teasdale, R. M., Gannon-Slater, N., La Londe, P. G., Crenshaw, H. L., Greene, J. C., & Schwandt, T. A. (2019). How did that happen? Teachers' explanations for low test scores. *Teachers College Record, 121*(2), 1–40.

Fisher, D., & Frey, N. (2015). Teacher modeling using complex informational texts. *The Reading Teacher, 69*(1), 63–69.

Fisher, D., & Frey, N. (2021). Rebuilding teacher efficacy. *Educational Leadership, 79*(3), 76–77.

Fisher, D., Frey, N., Almarode, J., Flories, K., & Nagel, D. (2020). *PLC+: Better decisions and greater impact by design*. Corwin.

Fisher, D., Frey, N., & Pumpian, I. (2012). *How to create a culture of achievement.* ASCD.

Garmston, R., Linder, C., & Whitaker, J. (1993). *Reflections on cognitive coaching.* ASCD.

Garmston, R. J., & Wellman, B. M. (1999). *The adaptive school: A sourcebook for developing collaborative groups.* Christopher Gordon.

Geller, A. (2021). *Should you cancel teacher data team meetings? You might be surprised.* https://www.smartbrief.com/original/2021/09/should-you-cancel-teacher-data-team-meetings-you-might-be-surprised

Goddard, R. D. (2001). Collective efficacy: A neglected construct in the study of schools and student achievement. *Journal of Educational Psychology, 93*(3), 467–476.

Goddard, R. D., Hoy, W. K., & Hoy, A. W. (2000). Collective teacher efficacy: Its meaning, measure, and impact on student achievement. *American Educational Research Journal, 37*(2), 479–507.

Hall, G., & Hord, S. (2015). *Implementing change: Patterns, principles and potholes* (4th ed.). Pearson.

Hattie, J. (2021). *Visible Learning Meta^X.* https://www.visiblelearningmetax.com

Hattie, J., & Zierer, C. (2018). *10 mindframes for Visible Learning.* Routledge.

Horn, I. S., & Little, J. W. (2010). Attending to problems of practice: Routines and resources for professional learning in teachers' workplace interactions. *American Educational Research Journal, 47*(1), 181–217.

Immordino-Yang, M. H. (2016). *Emotions, learning, and the brain.* W. W. Norton & Co.

Joyce, B. (2016). What are we learning about how we learn? *The Learning Professional.* https://learningforward.org/journal/june-2016-issue/what-are-we-learning-about-how-we-learn/

Joyce, B., & Calhoun, E. (2015). Beyond professional development. *Journal of Staff Development, 36*(6), 42–46.

Joyce, B., & Showers, B. (1982). The coaching of teaching. *Educational Leadership, 40*(1), 4–8.

Katzenmeyer, M., & Moller, G. (2009). *Awakening the sleeping giant: Helping teachers develop as leaders.* Corwin.

Klassen, R. M., Usher, E. L., & Bong, M. (2010). Teachers' collective efficacy, job satisfaction, and job stress in cross-cultural context. *Journal of Experimental Education, 78*, 464–486.

Kraft, M. A., Blazar, D., & Hogan, D. (2017). The effect of teaching coaching on instruction and achievement: A meta-analysis of the causal evidence. *Review of Educational Research, 88*(4), 547–588.

Kurz, S. L., & Knight, T. B. (2003). An exploration of the relationship among teacher efficacy, collective teacher efficacy, and goal consensus. *Learning Environments Research, 7*(2), 111–128.

Learning Forward. (2017). *Standards for the learning professional.* https://learningforward.org/standards/

Manz, C. C., & Sims Jr., H. P. (1981). Vicarious learning: The influence of modeling on organizational behavior. *Academy of Management Review, 6*(1), 105–113.

National School Reform Faculty. (n.d.). *NSRF protocols and activities.* https://nsrfharmony.org/protocols/

Pierce, S. (2019). The importance of building collective teacher efficacy. *Leadership Magazine.* https://leadership.acsa.org/building-teacher-efficacy

Protheroe, N. (2008). *Teacher efficacy: What is it and does it matter?* National Association of Elementary School Principles.

Quaglia, R. J., & Lande, L. L. (2017). *Teacher voice.* Corwin.

Salanova, M., Rodriguez Sanchez, A. M., Schaufeli, W. B., & Cifre, E. (2014). Flowing together: A longitudinal study of collective efficacy and collective flow among workgroups. *Journal of Psychology Interdisciplinary and Applied, 14*(8), 435–455.

Sawyer, R. K. (2003). *Group creativity: Music, theater, collaboration.* Lawrence Erlbaum Associates.

Sharratt, L., & Planche, B. (2016). *Leading collaborative learning: Empowering excellence.* Corwin.

Sparks, D. (2013). Strong teams, strong schools. *Learning Forward, 34*(2), 28–30.

Tschannen-Moran, M., & Barr, M. (2004). Fostering student learning: The relationship of collective teacher efficacy and student achievement. *Leadership and Policy and Schools, 3*(3), 189–209.

INDEX

CORWIN

A SAGE Publishing Company

Helping educators make the greatest impact

CORWIN HAS ONE MISSION: to enhance education through intentional professional learning.

We build long-term relationships with our authors, educators, clients, and associations who partner with us to develop and continuously improve the best evidence-based practices that establish and support lifelong learning.